# Basic Vocabulary *in use*

D1613939

60 units of
vocabulary
practice in
North American
English

**Second**
Edition

**with answers**

# Michael McCarthy
# Felicity O'Dell
## with Randi Reppen

CAMBRIDGE
UNIVERSITY PRESS

# CAMBRIDGE
## UNIVERSITY PRESS

79 Anson Road, #06-04/06, Singapore 079906

Cambridge University Press is part of the University of Cambridge.

It furthers the University's mission by disseminating knowledge in the pursuit of education, learning and research at the highest international levels of excellence.

www.cambridge.org
Information on this title : www.cambridge.org/9780521123679

First published 2001
Second edition 2010
5th printing 2014

Printed in Singapore by Craft Print International Ltd

ISBN 978-0-521-12367-9 paperback Basic Student's Book with answers
ISBN 978-0-521-12375-4 paperback Intermediate Student's Book with answers
ISBN 978-0-521-12386-0 paperback High Intermediate Student's Book with answers

# Contents

Acknowledgments      v
Introduction      vii

**Learner training**

1   Talking about language
2   Learning strategies

**Common verbs**

3   *Have*
4   *Go*
5   *Do*
6   *Make*
7   *Come*
8   *Take*
9   *Give*
10   *Get*
11   Phrasal verbs
12   Verbs for everyday actions
13   Verbs of talking
14   Verbs of movement

**Words and grammar**

15   Conjunctions and other connecting words
16   Time words
17   Describing time: when
18   Describing place: where
19   Describing manner: how
20   Irregular verbs
21   Common uncountable words
22   Adjectives describing good and bad things
23   Adjectives describing people
24   Words and prepositions
25   Prefixes
26   Suffixes
27   Greetings and other useful phrases
28   Words and phrases you may confuse

**People**

29   Birth, marriage, and death
30   The family
31   Parts of the body
32   Clothes
33   Describing people's appearance
34   Sickness and health
35   Feelings

**The world**

36 Countries, languages, and people
37 Weather
38 In the city
39 In the country
40 Pets and other animals
41 Travel
42 Signs and notices

**At home**

43 Food and drink
44 In the kitchen
45 In the bedroom and bathroom
46 In the living room

**School and workplace**

47 Jobs
48 School
49 Communications

**Leisure**

50 Taking a trip
51 Shopping
52 In a hotel
53 Eating out
54 Sports
55 Movies
56 Leisure at home

**Social issues**

57 Crime
58 The media
59 Everyday problems
60 Global problems

Common weights and measures     122
Phonetic symbols                123
List of irregular verbs         124
Index                           126
Answer key                      139

# Acknowledgments

We wish to thank the following reviewers, whose comments were so helpful in improving this book: Julien Park, English Language Academy, South Korea; Nick Taggert, Instructor, Interactive College of Technology, Chamblee, Georgia; and Nina Ito, Academic Coordinator, American Language Institute, California State University, U.S.A.

We also wish to acknowledge the insightful suggestions provided by reviewers at Cambridge University Press: Emeric Lau, Singapore; Jinhee Park, South Korea; Satoko Shimoyama, Japan; and Alex Martinez, Mexico.

But above all, we are indebted to our American adapter and *Corpus* consultant Randi Reppen, who made sure the text was faithful to contemporary American usage. Without Randi's collaboration, we would not be publishing this second edition.

Many thanks are due to the following editorial staff at Cambridge University Press: Ann Pascoe-van Zyl, Caitlin Mara, Katherine Wong, Kathleen O'Reilly, Keiko Sugiyama, and Richard Walker. Our special thanks go to Bernard Seal, who guided this book through the editorial process with his usual calm and professionalism.

Finally, we would like to thank all those who helped in the making of the first edition of *Basic Vocabulary in Use*, especially Ellen Shaw, our original American English adapter.

Michael McCarthy

Felicity O'Dell

November 2009

The authors and publishers would like to thank Rachel Wilson and Stephen Forster.

Layout and design:  Transnet Pte Ltd
                    based on a design by Tanky Media
Cover design:       Studioleng

Illustrations by Jamaika Sophie Wong Suk Fan, Jonathan C. Shih, LiDan Illustration & Design Studio, Patrick Niebres, and Tanky Media.

# Introduction

This new edition of *Basic Vocabulary in Use* still retains the features that made the first edition so popular:

- The format of presentation on the left-hand page and practice on the right-hand page.
- Approaching vocabulary in a variety of ways: topics (e.g., Eating out, Food and drink), common verbs (e.g., Phrasal verbs), words and grammar (e.g., Time words, Prefixes), etc.
- A student-friendly Answer key, including not only correct answers to right/wrong exercises, but also possible answers for more open-ended exercises.
- Usage notes that are ideal for self-study learners.
- A complete unit-by-unit Index, which lists all the target words and phrases.

## What is different about the new edition?

### Updated content

#### The content has been updated in several ways:

- A new design makes the book easier to use: language explanations are more clearly shown, example answers to the exercise questions are in a different color, and *tip* boxes are more clearly marked.
- All the artwork is new: illustrations are clearer and more attractive, and they reflect recent changes in technology.
- A new unit on the verb **give** has been added, focusing on its basic meaning and collocations.
- New words that have entered the language and become common have been added: for example, *text message* (Unit 49), *Wi-Fi* (Unit 52).
- Vocabulary explanations are clearer and more logically presented.
- Exercises have been updated and improved where possible: for example, in Unit 5, Exercise 5.1 better practices the use of **do** as a general verb.
- The Index is organized unit by unit, allowing learners to see at a glance the key words and phrases of any unit.

### Use of the *Cambridge English Corpus*

This new edition has made use of the *Cambridge English Corpus* of written and spoken English. This has been important in several ways:

- The *Corpus* has been used to check that all language and content is contemporary, natural, and accurate.
- The frequency information in the *Corpus* has helped guide the selection of words and phrases in the book and ensure that the vocabulary will be suitable for learners of English at a basic level.
- Example sentences are the same or similar to those in the *Corpus*. In other words, the examples show you words and phrases being used in their most typical contexts.

## Using this book

### Who is this book for?

*Basic Vocabulary in Use* has been written to help take learners from a very basic level of vocabulary to a level where they can use around 2,000 words and phrases. It has been designed for students who are studying on their own, but it can also be used by a teacher in the classroom with a group of students.

### How is the book organized?

The book has 60 two-page units. The left-hand page explains the new words and phrases chosen for that unit. Most units contain approximately 25 new words or phrases and they are all highlighted in **bold**. The right-hand page gives you a chance to check your understanding through a series of exercises which practice the new vocabulary.

The book is organized around everyday topics, but also has units devoted to core verbs such as **get** and **go**, as well as units concerned with ways of learning vocabulary. Typical errors are indicated where appropriate, and the most common meanings and uses are focused on for each key item.

There is an Answer key at the back of the book. This gives correct answers to exercises with "right" or "wrong" solutions, and also possible answers for exercises which do not have "right" or "wrong" solutions.

There is also an Index at the back of the book. This lists all the words and phrases introduced in the book. It is organized unit by unit.

### The left-hand page

The left-hand page introduces the new vocabulary for each topic or area of language. The vocabulary is divided into a number of sections (A, B, C, etc.) with simple, clear titles. New words and phrases are explained in a number of different ways:

1. A short definition
   e.g., a **date** [a romantic meeting]; **do the laundry** [wash clothes]; **apologize** [say "I'm sorry."]

2. A short explanation
   e.g., What topics **came up** in class today? [What topics did you talk about?]

3. Example sentences
   For many new words, sentence examples give a situation that helps you understand the meaning:
   Some people cannot find jobs and are **unemployed**.
   I need some coins for the parking meter. Do you have any **change**?

4. A picture or diagram
   This is the clearest way to illustrate a large number of words.

   e.g.,   **lightning**                **surprised**                **swim**

### The right-hand page

The right-hand page contains the exercises to practice the new vocabulary presented on the left-hand page. There are a variety of activity types, ranging from traditional activities such as fill-in-the-blanks, to more open-ended ones. There are also personalized activities which enable learners to talk about their lives. Although the activities are designed for self-study, they can easily be adapted for pair work, group work, or whole-class activities.

### How should I use the book?

The units in the book can be used in any order you like, but we recommend you do the first two units on learning vocabulary first. As well as teaching you important words and phrases, they will give you information about vocabulary and also ideas and techniques to help you learn vocabulary.

Everything you need is in the book. The new vocabulary is explained on the left-hand page, and the exercises have an Answer key at the back of the book. But if you need a dictionary to help you with any of the words and phrases, or exercises, you can go to http://dictionary.cambridge.org/, where you can look up words you are not sure of and learn more about words you already know.

### Companion Web site:   www.cambridge.org/vinu

On the *Vocabulary in Use* Companion Web site, you will find a range of free additional activities for vocabulary and listening practice.

We hope you like this book. When you have finished it, you can go to the next book in the series, *Vocabulary in Use Intermediate*, and after that, to the highest level, *Vocabulary in Use High Intermediate*.

Good luck!

# Talking about language

### A Language words

| Part of speech | Meaning | Examples |
|---|---|---|
| noun | a person, place, or thing | Mary, China, pen |
| verb | something we do | eat, read, write |
| adjective | describes a noun | good, bad, happy, long |
| adverb | describes a verb | slowly, badly, well |
| preposition | used before a noun | in, on, by, at, of |

| Other useful concepts | Meaning | Examples |
|---|---|---|
| singular | one noun | book, house, child |
| plural | more than one noun | books, houses, children |
| phrase | a group of words (not a complete sentence) | in a house, at home, an old man |
| sentence | a complete idea; begins with a capital letter and ends with a period | The new student parked his car in front of the school. |
| paragraph | one or more sentences about the same topic beginning on a new line | *Basic Vocabulary in Use* has 60 units. Each unit has has two pages. |
| question | a group of words that begins with a capital letter and ends with a question mark | What time is it? Do you speak Spanish? |

### B Instructions used in this book

1. **Match the words on the left with the words on the right.**
   orange    ice cream
   chocolate    juice
2. **Fill in the blank.**
   Maria is ....... *at* ....... home today.
3. **Correct the mistakes.**
   Maria is in home today. .*Maria is at home today.*...
4. **Complete the sentence about yourself.**
   I take ...*the bus*... to work.
5. **Write these words in the correct column.**

   | cat    apples    oranges    dog    horse |
   |---|

   | Animals | Fruits |
   |---|---|
   | cat, dog, horse | apples, oranges |

# Exercises

**1.1**   Write these words in the correct column.

| shirt | quietly | of | speak | by | quickly | bad | car | banana | at |
|-------|---------|-----|-------|-----|---------|-----|-----|--------|-----|
| daily | write | new | in | woman | old | sad | eat | correctly | go |

| Noun | Verb | Adjective | Adverb | Preposition |
|------|------|-----------|--------|-------------|
| *shirt* | | | | |
| | | | | |
| | | | | |

**1.2**   Are these phrases, sentences, or questions?

1. in the park .*phrase*............
2. Do you speak English? ........................
3. a black cat ........................
4. She's writing a book. ........................
5. What's your name? ........................
6. I like English. ........................

**1.3**   Answer these questions.

1. What is the plural of *book*? ..*books*............
2. What is the singular of *women*? ........................
3. Is *from* a verb? ........................
4. Is *cat* an adjective? ........................
5. Is this a phrase: "Jane loves Harry."? ........................

**1.4**   Follow these instructions.

1. Fill in the blank. What ........................................ your name?
2. Complete the sentence about yourself. I have ........................................eyes.
3. Correct the mistakes.
   speek ........................................................
   inglish ........................................................
   He has seven cat ........................................................
4. Match the verbs on the left with the nouns on the right.
   make             homework
   do                a shower
   take            a mistake
5. Write these words in the correct column:

   hat      rice      coat      milk

| Food | Clothes |
|------|---------|
| | |

# Learning strategies

**A** **Write down words that go together (collocations).**

You **do the exercises** in this book. Sometimes, you **make mistakes** in English. In your vocabulary notebook, write: **do + exercise** and **make + mistake**.

When words are used together like this, we call it a **collocation**.

You **make mistakes**. (*not* ~~do~~ mistakes)                    verb + noun
I'm **on the bus**. (*not* ~~in~~ the bus)                        preposition + noun
Some people are **good at** languages. (*not* good ~~in~~)        adjective + preposition
I saw a very **tall man**. (*not* ~~high~~ man)                   adjective + noun

**B** **Learn words in groups that are related (word families).**

| Word family | Some words in the family |
|---|---|
| furniture | chair, desk, table, sofa |
| travel | ticket, passport, visa, bus |

**C** **Pictures and diagrams**

Draw pictures in your notebook to help remember words. For example: **car**

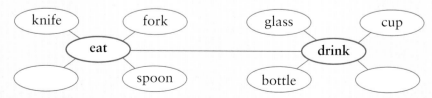

windshield — trunk — window — door — tire — headlight

Draw diagrams like this one. Add more words as you learn them.

knife    fork        glass    cup

eat ——————————— drink

spoon        bottle

# Exercises

**2.1** How many more collocations for *have* + noun can you write in your vocabulary notebook? Look at Unit 3 for more ideas.

*have a party, have lunch,* ...........................................................................................................................

**2.2** Not all of the words listed in the box describe weather. Which words can go with *weather*? Use a dictionary if you need help.

| wet | high | big | dry | warm | happy | cool | rainy | light |

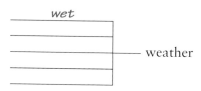

— weather

**2.3** Write these words in the correct family. Use a dictionary if you need help.

| school | bread | teacher | milk | notebook | test | water | salad | student | rice |

| Name of word family | Words in family |
|---|---|
| education | |
| food | |

**2.4** Draw simple pictures to help you remember the words in bold.

*Example:* a girl **crying**

1. a plane **lands**
2. **sunny** weather
3. **under** the table

**2.5** Write words in the empty circles.

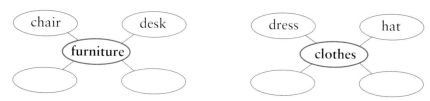

> **tip**  *Make sure you have started a vocabulary notebook before you do the other units in this book.*

# *Have*

**A** *Have*

**Have** often means *to own* or *possess*.
 I **have** a computer.
 We **have** a small house.
 I **don't have** enough money to buy a car.

**B** What can you *have*?

You can . . .
 **have** breakfast.
 **have** a party.
 **have** a class.
 **have** a cup of coffee/tea.
 **have** a cold (when you're sick).

**C** Other things you can *have*

| *Example* | *Other things* |
|---|---|
| breakfast | dinner, lunch, a meal, something to eat |
| a party | a meeting, a date [a romantic meeting], a good time, an argument |
| a class | homework, a test, an exam, an appointment (with the dentist) |
| a cup of coffee/tea | something to drink, a drink, a snack [a little food between meals] |
| a cold | the flu, a headache, a broken arm, a sore throat |

**D** Expressions with *have*

**Have a nice day.**
Goodbye! **Have a good trip!** [when someone is going away]
**I have a brother and two sisters.**
She's going to **have a baby** [give birth] next month.
I want to learn to ski, but **I don't have time.**
Do you ever **have trouble / have problems** [difficulty]
 understanding English?

**E** *Have to = must*

Use **have to** when something is necessary and you have no choice.
 The museum isn't free. You **have to** pay $10 to get in.
 She **has to** take an exam at the end of the course.

MUSEUM
ENTRANCE
🏛 **$10**

Use **don't have to** when something is not necessary and you have a choice.
 **I don't have to** work on Saturdays.
 We **don't have to** go to the party if you don't want to.

# Exercises

**3.1    Fill in the blanks. Use words from B, C, and D on page 6.**

1. I never have a big ....*breakfast*.... in the morning.
2. I have an ........................ with the doctor at 1 o'clock.
3. I had a ........................ yesterday, so I studied all night.
4. Mike is having a ........................ on Saturday night. Are you going?
5. I'm too busy, so  I don't have ........................ to take a vacation.
6. I have a terrible ........................ . I keep sneezing. Atchoo!
7. I had a ........................ with Maria last night. We went out to dinner and a movie.
8. Keiko is going to have a ........................ . She thinks it'll be a girl.

**3.2    Answer these questions about yourself.**

1. Do you have any brothers or sisters? If yes, how many?
2. Which days do you have classes?
3. What do you usually have for lunch?
4. On weekends do you have to get up early in the morning?
5. Do you have coffee or tea with breakfast?
6. Is there anything you don't have at home that you want to have? What is it?
7. Do you ever have trouble understanding English? When?
8. Do you have to study hard to learn English?

**3.3    Do the crossword puzzle.**

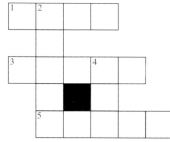

Across
1. You can have one in a restaurant.
3. Some people like to have one on New Year's Eve.
5. You have this between meals.

Down
2. You have these at school.
4. If you don't want coffee, you can have ................ .

**3.4    Complete the sentences using *have*.**

1. A: I'm thirsty!
   B: Why don't you ........................................ ?
2. A: I feel sick today.
   B: Do you........................................ ?
3. A: Bye, everyone! I'm leaving for my trip to Hawaii!
   B: Bye, ........................................ !
4. A: Can you come to my party on Friday?
   B: I can't. I have a big test on Monday, and I ........................................ this weekend.

# Unit 4    *Go*

## A    *Go*

Go means to move from one place to another.
I **go** home after school. Ahmed **goes** to work after school.
Where **does** this road **go**?
Is this bus **going** downtown?
Let's **go** to the movies tonight.
We **went** to Mexico last summer.
(went = past tense of go)

## B    *Go* + prepositions

Many prepositions can follow **go**, such as **to**, **out**, **up** and **down**.

Kim **went to**
her room.

Kanako **went out**
the door.

Paulo **went up**
the stairs slowly.

Ann **went down**
the stairs quickly.

## C    *Go* + *-ing* for activities

Use **go** with **-ing** for certain activities.

I hate to **go shopping**.

I usually **go swimming**
in the morning.

Let's **go dancing**.

Do you want to
**go sightseeing?**

Mei **goes skiing**
in the winter.

Bob is **going
fishing** today.

## D    Future plans with *be going to*

On Saturday John **is going to** visit his aunt. On Sunday we **are going to** stay at home. On Monday **I'm going to** meet Sam for lunch.

8

# Exercises

**4.1**  **Where are they going? What are they going to do? Write two sentences.**

1. Bill *is going to the club. He is going to go dancing.*
2. Jean and Mike ........................................................................................................ .
3. Antonio ............................................................................................................... .
4. The Lees ............................................................................................................. .
5. Sun-hee ............................................................................................................. .

**4.2**  **Correct the mistakes.**

1. I went Brazil. *I went to Brazil.* ................................................................................
2. We're going sightsee today. ......................................................................................
3. Joe went down to the top of the hill. ..........................................................................
4. Where this bus go?. ................................................................................................
5. Sarah goed out to dinner. .........................................................................................

**4.3**  **Write about Sue's plans for next week.**
**Use *be going to*.**

1. On Monday *Sue is going to play tennis with Rose.* .......................................................
2. On Tuesday .......................................................................................................... .
3. On Wednesday ...................................................................................................... .
4. On Thursday ......................................................................................................... .
5. On Friday ............................................................................................................ .

**4.4**  **Look at the activities in C on page 8. Which activities do you do on vacation?**
**Write sentences.**

*I usually go shopping when I'm on vacation.*

9

### A What are you *doing*?

A: What are the people in the picture **doing**?
B: They're dancing.

A: What do you **do** to relax?
B: I listen to music.

Don't **do** that, Tommy.

### B *Do* + task

**do** the housework [clean the home]
**do** the laundry [wash clothes]
**do** the dishes [wash dishes]
**do** the cooking
**do** business with
**do** (your) homework

A: Did you **do the dishes** this morning?
B: No, I'm going to **do** them later.

Our company **does a lot of business with** Canada.
You always **do a good job**.

### C What *do* you *do*? [What is your job?]

What **do** you **do**? [What is your job?]
   I'm a student.    *or*    I'm a teacher.    *or*    I'm an engineer.
What does your wife **do**? [What is your wife's job?]
   She's a lawyer.    *or*    She's a secretary.    *or*    She's a doctor.

### D *Do* used with other verbs

|  | *Simple present* | *Simple past* |
|---|---|---|
| Questions | **Do** you like tennis? | **Did** they like the movie? |
| Short answers | Yes, I **do**.<br>So **does** Mari. | Yes, they **did**.<br>So **did** I. |
| Negatives | He **doesn't play** well. | Bob **didn't see** it. |

> *tip*    *Write down expressions with **do** that you find when you are reading in English. (See Unit 6 for differences between **do** and **make**.)*

# Exercises

**5.1**   Answer these questions about the people in the house. Use *do* in the sentence.

1.  What is the man doing? ....*He is doing the dishes.*....
2.  What is the woman doing? ................................................
3.  What are the girls doing? ................................................
4.  What are the boys doing? ................................................
5.  What is Grandpa doing?................................................

**5.2**   Write questions and answers about the jobs of the people in the pictures.

      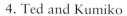

1.  *What does Lara Brown do? She's a secretary.*.................
2.  ................................................
3.  ................................................
4.  ................................................

**5.3**   Answer these questions about yourself. Use short answers with *do* as an auxiliary.

1.  Did you go to the movies last night? .*Yes, I did.*..........
2.  Do your parents live near you? ................................................
3.  Do you have blue eyes? ................................................
4.  Did you eat lunch with friends yesterday? ................................................
5.  Does your kitchen have a microwave? ................................................
6.  Did you take a vacation last year? ................................................

**5.4**   Look at the *do* expressions in B on page 10. Write sentences about you or your family and these activities.

*I usually do the cooking at home, but I never do the laundry.*

# Make

## A Make . . . (food and drinks)

to **make coffee**

to **make dinner / a meal**

I'll **make** some **tea/soup**.
I **make breakfast/lunch/dinner** every day.

## B Make a . . .

She's **making a call /
a phone call.**

He's **making a copy.**

She's **making
a video.**

## C Don't make mistakes with *make*!

| Can I say . . . ? | Yes/No | Correction |
|---|---|---|
| I **made** a mistake in the exercise. | ✓ | |
| I have to ~~make~~ my homework. | ✗ | I have to **do** my homework. |
| I have to ~~make~~ a test next week. | ✗ | I have to **take** a test next week. |
| Do you want to stay or go? You have to **make** a decision [decide]. | ✓ | |
| I have to **make** an appointment with the doctor/dentist/teacher. [set up a time to see that person] | ✓ | |
| I'd like to ~~make~~ a picture of you. | ✗ | I'd like to **take** a picture of you. |
| After dinner I'll ~~make~~ the dishes. | ✗ | After dinner I'll **do** the dishes. |

## D It *makes* me (feel) . . .

Flying always **makes me (feel)** nervous.
My friend called me stupid. It **made me (feel)** really angry.
That movie **made me (feel)** so sad.

# Exercises

**6.1** Fill in the blanks with *make* or *do*.

1. I always ......*make*.......... mistakes when I speak English.
2. Let's go to bed now. We can ........................ the dishes in the morning.
3. I'm going to ........................ some coffee. Do you want a cup?
4. Kris always ........................ lots of phone calls in the evening.
5. If I ........................ my homework every day, my English will improve.

**6.2** Complete the sentences with *make(s) me (feel)* or *made me (feel)*.

1. That movie ........................ sad.
2. Tests always ........................ nervous.
3. The waiter wasn't very nice to me. It ........................ angry.
4. You were so nice to me. You ........................ very welcome.

**6.3** What are these people doing? Complete the sentences with *make*.

1. She's ........................ .

3. He's ........................ .

2. She's ........................ .

4. They're ........................ .

**6.4** Correct the mistakes.

1. I have to ~~make~~ my homework.   *I have to do my homework.*
2. Can I make a picture of you?
3. He's 35, but he never makes his own laundry. He takes his dirty clothes to his mother's.
4. I have to take an appointment with the dentist.
5. Do students have to make a test at the end of their English course?
6. We have to do a decision today.

**A** *Come and go are different.*

HERE ⟵ come      HERE ⟶ go ⟶ THERE

**B** *Come in and come out*

*Come in!*

You can say "**Come in!**" when someone knocks at the door of a room. Then the person who knocked **comes into** the room.

You put your card in, and the money **comes out** of the ATM.

**C** **Other expressions with *come***

**Come back** means return to the same place.
    She went away for three days. She **came back** yesterday. [She is here again.]
    **Come back** to this unit and review the words.

Can I **come over** [visit] and see you tonight?
He **came from** Mexico to visit his brother.

A: **Come on**, let's go to the movies!
B: I can't go with you.

A: **How come?** [Why is that?]
B: My friend is **coming over**.

> **tip**    *Write down any prepositions you find with **come** every time you see them.*

# Exercises

**7.1**   Fill in the blanks with words from page 14.

1. I put money in, but the money didn't come .....*out of*..... the ATM.
2. A: ......................................... here!
   B: No, I don't want to ......................................... there!
3. A: I'm going to Hawaii tomorrow.
   B: Oh! When are you coming ......................................... ?
   A: In two weeks.
4. A: Sara, are you home?
   B: Yes, come ......................................... .
5. A: I'll be home late tonight.
   B: Oh, really? How ......................................... ?
   A: Because I have to work late.
6. When will Terry come ......................................... for pizza?
7. Come ......................................... ! We have to hurry.

**7.2**   What do you think these people are saying?

1. .........................................

2. .........................................

**7.3**   Fill in the blanks using *come* in the correct form.

1. ......................... on we'll miss the bus.
2. She ......................... over for dinner last night.
3. He ......................... here every Tuesday.
4. We're having a party. Do you want to ......................... ?
5. I put money in the machine, and a candy bar ......................... out.

## *Take*

**A**   *Take* **with time**    it + takes + (person) + time

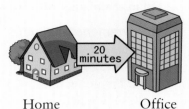

It **takes** me 20 minutes to get to work.
home → 20 minutes → office

Home          Office

I go to school/class every day. It **takes** 30 minutes.
I do homework every day. It **took** me two hours yesterday.

A: How long does it **take** to get to the airport?
B: An hour by taxi.

**B**   *Take* **with bus, train, etc.**

A: How do you get to work?
B: I **take** the bus.

In New York you can **take the subway**
to Central Park.

**C**   *Take* **with classes, tests, etc.**

A: Are you **taking** an English class?
B: Yes.

A: Do you have to **take** many tests?
B: Yes, one every week.

I want to **take** Spanish lessons.

She **took** a course in art history last summer.

**D**   *Take* **something with you**

Are you going out? **Take** an umbrella.
It's raining.

Are you going to the beach?
**Take** some sunscreen with you.

I'm sorry, but you can't **take** your camera
into the museum.

**E**   **Other useful expressions with** *take*

Can I **take your picture**?
I need to **take medicine** for my allergies.
Every morning I **take a shower**.
Betty still **takes a nap** after lunch.

# Exercises

**8.1** Look at the pictures. Answer the questions using *take*.

1. How does Mariko go to work?
   She ..................................... .
   It .................... her 20 minutes
   to get to work.

3. How do I get to the airport?
   You .................................. .
   It .................... one hour to get from
   your hotel to the airport.

2. How does Jack go to school?
   He .......................................... .

4. How do Pedro and Ana get home?
   They .......................................... .

**8.2** Complete the sentences using *take/took/taking* and an expression from the box.

> a course   yoga lessons   any classes   a test

1. Are you .......................................... this semester?
2. I wanted to learn a foreign language, so I .......................................... in Chinese.
3. Every Monday I have to .......................................... , so I study on the weekends.
4. Last year I .......................................... . It really helped me to relax.

**8.3** What do you *take* in these situations?

1. You want to take pictures. ...*I take a camera*...........

2. You want to get yourself clean. .....................................

3. You travel to another country. .....................................

4. You have a cold. .....................................

5. You are tired. .....................................

**8.4** How long did it take you to do this unit?

.......................................................................................

# Give

## A  *Give* someone something

We **give** someone something. **Give** needs two objects: someone who receives something, and something that the person receives.

| | Someone | Something | |
|---|---|---|---|
| I **gave** | my sister | a book | for her birthday. |
| She **gives** | us | vegetables | from her garden. |

## B  *Give* something *to* someone

We can also put the thing before the person who receives it. Then we use *to* + receiver.

Tammy **gave** a message **to** Joan.

If we use a pronoun (e.g., *it*, *them*) for the thing we **give**, we must use the pronoun first and then *to* + receiver.

| | Something | Someone |
|---|---|---|
| He gave | it | to his cousin. |
| I usually give | them | to my friends. |

A: What did he do with **the camera**?
B: He gave **it** *to his cousin*.
(*not* he gave his cousin it).

A: What do you do with your old **books**?
B: I usually give **them** *to my friends*.

## C  Common collocations with *give*

Give me a call.
Did you **give Yumiko my number**?
Please **give a message** to Allen.
Can you **give me some advice**?
Please **give Scott directions** to your house.
I **gave him money** for the movies.
Did you **give Ali permission** to ride your bike?
Did they **give an explanation for** why they were late?

## D  Common phrasal verbs and idioms with *give*

I **gave back** [returned] the pen I borrowed.
I want to **give up** eating candy. [stop doing something]
**Give me a break,** [give me a chance / be nice] I'm doing my best.
Can you **give me a hand** [help me] with this box?

# Exercises

**9.1** Look at the pictures and write a sentence.

1. *Aunt Julie gave Bella a CD*
   *for her birthday.*

3. ............................................................

2. ............................................................

4. ............................................................

**9.2** Look at the pictures in 9.1 again and answer the questions. Be sure to use a pronoun.

1. Who did Aunt Julie give the CD to? *She gave it to Bella.*
2. Who did Grandmother give the camera to?
3. Who did Tony give the chocolates to?
4. Who did Sam give the flowers to?

**9.3** Replace the underlined words with one of the collocations with *give* from C on page 18. Write a new sentence.

1. Could you <u>tell me how to get to</u> the new sports club?
   *Could you give me directions to the new sports club?*
2. <u>Call me</u> on Saturday.
3. I don't know what to do. Please <u>advise me</u>.
4. They'll never <u>permit you</u> to take so many books out of the library.
5. When you e-mail Maria don't forget to <u>explain</u> why you can't go to her party.

**9.4** Complete these sentences with words from the box.

> money   e-mail address   number   message   examples

1. Did you give your brother some .............................. for the movies?
2. I need to phone Paco this evening. Could you give me his new .............................. ?
3. Could you give Jenny a .............................., please? Tell her we're meeting at 7.30.
4. It's a great book. It gives me .............................. of jokes from different countries.
5. I lost contact with her, but then a friend gave me her .............................. .

**9.5** Complete each sentence with a phrasal verb or an idiom from D on page 18.

1. I need some help. Could you .............................. with my homework?
2. I'm going to .............................. watching TV and get more exercise.
3. I don't need these boxes anymore. I'd like to .............. them .............. .
4. When you finish my book, please .............. it .............. to me.
5. ..............................! Turn the music down, I'm trying to study.

**A** *Get* with adjectives: for changes

It's light. → It's getting dark. → It's dark.

He's **getting** tired.
He wants to go to bed.

It's raining!
She's **getting** wet!

She's **getting ready** to go to work.

**B** *Get* with nouns

If you don't have something, you can **get** [obtain, find, or receive] it.
   I want to **get** an A on my test.
   I've finished school. Now I want to **get** a job.
   I'm going to the store to **get** some fruit.

**C** *Get to* [arrive at / reach] a place

A: How can I **get to** the airport?
B: Take the airport bus.

A: When you **get to** São Paulo, call me.
B: OK, give me your number.

**D** Other phrases with *get*

Maria and David are **getting married** in June.
When you **get back** [return / come home] from Hong Kong,
   call me.
When **I get home**, I take off my shoes. (*not* get ~~to~~ home)
I'll probably **get there** at 6 o'clock, so please call
   me at 6:30. (*not* get ~~to~~ there)
I want to **get a haircut**.

# Exercises

**10.1** Complete these sentences using *getting* and a word from the box.

| | |
|---|---|
| ready | 1. A storm is coming. *It's getting dark.* |
| light | 2. The sun is coming up, it ................................................ |
| dark | 3. It's almost time for school! He ................................. |
| cold | 4. It's raining! I .......................................................! |
| wet | 5. Please close the window. I .................................... |

**10.2** What do you do in the following situations? Be sure to use *get*.

1. You want to mail a postcard. *I get a stamp.*
2. You want to earn some money. ................................................
3. You want to write something down. .........................................
4. Your hair is too long. ..............................................................
5. You want to have something hot to drink. ...............................

**10.3** Write what's happening in each picture.

1. *She got tired.*

4. .................................................................

university
(25 minutes)
my house

2. .................................................................

5. .................................................................

3. .................................................................

**10.4** Answer these questions.

1. In your country, how old are people (usually) when they get married?
2. When do most people get married? Which day? Which month(s)?
3. What time do you get home every day?
4. How do you get home from school/work?

### A    What are phrasal verbs?

Phrasal verbs have two parts:
a verb (e.g., *get, go*) + a preposition (e.g., *up, on*).
*get up/along*
I **got up** at 6:30 this morning. I'm tired now.
My sister and I **get along** very well. [are very friendly]

| get | over a cold |
|---|---|
| | up at 6:30 |
| | along with my sister |

*turn on/off/up/down*
He always **turns on** the TV at 10 o'clock to
    watch the news.
It's a sunny day. **Turn off** the light.
**Turn up** the TV. I can't hear it.
**Turn down** the TV. It's too loud.

*Turn down the TV!*

*go on/off*
What's **going on** here? [What's happening?]
My alarm clock **went off** [rang; made noise] at 7 a.m.

*Come on! We're late.*

*come on/up*
**Come on!** [Hurry!] We're late.
What topics **came up** in class today? [What topics did you talk about?]

*put on* (clothes)
It's cold and windy outside. **Put on** your coat.

*give up*
Don't **give up!** [stop trying] You will learn to use phrasal verbs.

### B    One phrasal verb, different meanings

*turn down*
She **turned down** the stereo. [made it not so loud]
She **turned down** the invitation. [refused it]

*take off*

The plane **takes off** at 12:30.
[departs or leaves the ground]

He **took off** his shoes.
[removed them from his feet]

---

**tip**    *Write down any phrasal verbs you see or hear on a special page in your notebook.*

# Exercises

**11.1**   **Match a sentence on the left with a sentence on the right.**

1. The alarm clock rang.
2. The news is on soon.
3. I'm trying to work.
4. It's snowing today.
5. I don't want to take that job.

a. I'll turn it down.
b. Please turn down that music.
c. It's time to get up.
d. Put on your coat.
e. Turn on the TV.

**11.2**   **Complete these sentences with the correct prepositions.**

1. It's dark in here. Turn ..........*on*.......... the lights.
2. Our plane takes ......................... at 6:25 and lands at 7:50.
3. Come ......................... ! It's time to get ......................... .
4. The children took ......................... their school uniforms when they got home.
5. It's time to turn ......................... the TV and go to bed now.
6. My friends and I always get ......................... well.
7. The subject of money always comes ......................... when he talks to his parents.
8. When they got to the beach, she put ......................... her swimsuit and ran down to the water.

**11.3**   **What is going on in these pictures? Use one of the phrasal verbs from page 22 to describe each picture.**

1. *The plane is taking off.*

3. .................................................

2. .................................................

4. .................................................

**11.4**   **Replace the underlined words with a phrasal verb from the box.**

took off   gave up   turn up   going on   got up   turned down

1. I <u>removed</u> my hat and coat.   *took off*

2. What's <u>happening</u> here?

3. <u>Make</u> the music <u>louder</u>. I can't hear it.

4. I <u>refused</u> the invitation to dinner.

5. I <u>left my bed</u> at 7:00 this morning.

6. I <u>stopped trying</u>.

# Verbs for everyday actions

**A** Things you do every day

I wake up

get up

take a shower

have breakfast

listen to music

go to work

come home

check e-mail

make dinner

call a friend

watch TV

go to sleep

**B** Sometimes I . . .

do the laundry

clean the house

go for a walk

surf the Internet

**C** Usually / Normally (what I do typically)

I **usually** get up at 8 o'clock.
  (*not* I'm used to get up at 8 o'clock.)

I **normally** drive to work.

**D** Questions about everyday things

**How often do you** check your e-mail / watch TV?
  Three times a week. / Every day.
**What time / When do you** get up / go to work?
  Seven o'clock. / 8:30.
**How do you** get to work?
  **I take** the bus/train.   *or*   I drive/walk.

# Exercises

**12.1** Complete the sentences using these words.

| wake up | go | take | have | do |
|---------|-----|------|------|-----|

1. Tony .....*wakes up*..... at 6:00 a.m. on weekdays.
2. He usually ......................................... coffee and toast for breakfast.
3. Normally he ......................................... to work at 8:00 a.m.
4. Sometimes he ......................................... the laundry at night.
5. He ......................................... a shower every day.

**12.2** What do they do? Complete the sentences.

1. He *checks his* ..........
   *e-mail every day.* .....
   (every day)

3. She c ......................
   ............................... .
   (every weekend)

5. She g ......................
   ............................... .
   (every morning)

2. He d ......................
   ............................... .
   (every Saturday)

4. He ......................
   w ........................... .
   (sometimes)

**12.3** Ask and answer these questions.

| Topic | Question | Answer |
|-------|----------|--------|
| 1. go to work | How *do you get to work?* | *I usually take the train.* |
| 2. go to sleep | What ...............................<br>........................................ ? | |
| 3. check your e-mail | When...............................<br>........................................ ? | |
| 4. surf the Internet | How often........................<br>........................................ ? | |

25

# Verbs of talking

### A  Say

Use **say** when you report someone's words.
> She **said**, "This is terrible!"
> He **said** (that) he wanted some coffee.

Use **say** when you ask about language.
> A:  **How do you say** "book" in Spanish?
> B:  "*Libro.*"

We **say hello/goodbye, please / thank you,
Happy Birthday / Happy New Year / Congratulations.**

### B  Tell

**Tell** is usually followed immediately by a person (e.g., **tell** me, him, her).
> He **told me** his name. (*not* He ~~said me~~ his name.)
Use **tell** when you want to know how to get to a place.
> **Can you tell me** where the post office is? (*not* Can you ~~say me~~ …?)

Use **tell** with other **wh**-words, too (**when, how, why, where**), e.g., you can **tell
someone how** to do something, **where** something is, **why** something happened.
> He **told me how** to send a fax. **Tell me when** you want to go home.

You can **tell someone the time / a story / a joke / your name / your age / your e-mail
address / a phone number / an address.**

### C  Ask

**Ask** is used for questions.
> My sister **asked me** where I was going.   *or*   My sister asked (me), "Where are
> you going?"

You can **ask someone a question / for the time.
Ask someone to do something,** and **ask someone
for something.**
> I **asked him to** turn off the music.
> She **asked** the waiter **for** the check.

### D  Speak / Talk / Answer

Note the different uses of these verbs:
> Do you **speak** Korean? (*not* Do you ~~talk~~ Korean?)
> I like **talking to** you.
> I'll **answer** the phone / the door.
> I sent him an e-mail, but he didn't **answer**.  *or*
> He didn't **answer** my e-mail.
> [He did not send me an e-mail back.]

# Exercises

**13.1** **Fill in the blanks with the correct form of *say* or *tell*.**

1. The police officer ..........*said*......... "Come here!"
2. She ........................ me her name.
3. I ........................ goodbye to him.
4. The little boy ........................ , "Please ........................ me a story."
5. Can you ........................ me where the Park Hotel is, please?
6. The teacher ........................ that the students were very good.

**13.2** **What do you say in these situations?**

1. You want to know where the
   subway station is.
   Can ...*you tell me where*...... 
   ...*the subway station is?*....

2. You want to know the word for "tea" in Chinese.
   How ................................................................ ?

3. You want to know the time.
   Excuse me, can you ................................................ ?

4. You want to know when the test is.
   Can you ................................................................ ?

5. You want to find someone who speaks English.
   Do you ................................................................ ?

**13.3** **Circle the correct verb to complete the phrases.**

1. Ask / (Tell) / Say          someone a joke
2. Talk / Speak / Say          "house" in German
3. Answer / Ask for / Ask      the check
4. Answer / Speak / Ask        an e-mail
5. Tell / Say / Speak          Happy Birthday
6. Talk / Speak / Talk to      a friend
7. Ask / Say / Talk            someone to help you

**13.4** **Fill in the blanks with *say* or *ask*. Then match the questions on the left with the answers on the right.**

1. How do you ........................ how much      a. *La cuenta, por favor!*
   something costs in Malay?

2. How do you ........................ "Hello"        b. *Berapa ini?*
   in Japanese?

3. How do you ........................ for the         c. *Feliz Ano Novo!*
   check in Spanish?

4. How do you ........................                  d. *Konnichi wa.*
   "Happy New Year!" in Portuguese?

# Verbs of movement

**A** Without transportation

walk        swim        climb        run        dance        fall        jump        jog

**B** Transportation

You **take** a bus / train / taxi / plane, and you **take** the subway.

You **ride** a bicycle / train / motorcycle / horse.

You **drive** a car / bus / taxi / truck.

The pilot **flies** a plane.

A: How did you get to Mexico City?
B: We **flew** there.

If you **catch** the bus, train, or plane, you arrive on time to get it.
If you **miss** the bus, train, or plane, you arrive too late to get it.

You **arrive in** or **at** a place. (*not* ~~to~~ a place)
    The train **arrived in** Tokyo on time.
    The plane **arrived at** Kennedy Airport two hours late.

**C** Moving objects

*Could you pass me the salt?*

*Can I help you carry your luggage?*

pull        push                pass                        carry

# Exercises

**14.1**  **Fill in the blanks with verbs from A on page 28. Use the correct form.**

1. Jack likes to ..........*jog*.......... around the park every morning.
2. Everyone ......................... at the party last night.
3. Every morning Alicia ......................... in the pool before breakfast.
4. Ana can ......................... very fast. She has won a lot of races.
5. Roberto likes to ......................... mountains.
6. My grandmother ......................... on her way home and broke her arm.
7. The cat ......................... off the table.
8. It is much better for you to ......................... to work than to drive or take the bus.

**14.2**  **Complete the sentences with *ride*, *drive*, *fly*, or *take*.**

1. Do you know how to ........*drive*.......... a car?
2. He works for an airline. He ......................... a plane.
3. I usually ......................... a taxi when it rains.
4. She ......................... a truck.
5. I prefer to ......................... the bus.
6. Would you like to ......................... an elephant?

**14.3**  **Answer these questions. Use answers like *every day*, *twice a week*, *once a year*, or *never*.**

1. How often do you walk to work or school? *I walk to work every day.* .
2. Do you have a bicycle? How often do you ride it?
3. How often do you swim? Do you swim in the ocean or in a swimming pool?
4. How often do you jog?
5. How often do you drive a car?
6. How often do you take a bus?

**14.4**  **Connect the objects to the verbs.**

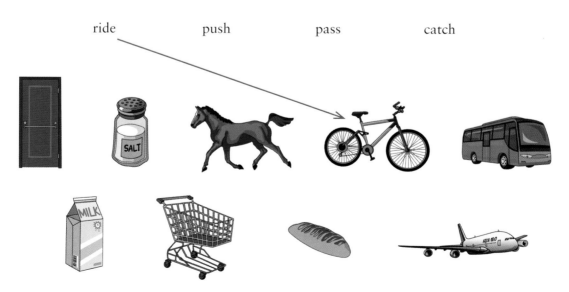

# Conjunctions and other connecting words

## A Conjunctions

Conjunctions join two parts of a sentence and help to show the connection between them. Note the use of commas before some conjunctions.

| Conjunction | Function | Example |
| --- | --- | --- |
| and | tells you more | We got home **and** went to bed. |
| but | shows a contrast | They are rich, **but** they aren't happy. |
| because | answers the question *why?* | We went home **because** we were tired. |
| so | tells you the result | We went home early, **so** we missed the end of the concert. |
| when | answers the questions *when* or *what time?* | We went home **when** it started to rain. |
| before | answers the question *what happened first?* | We went home **before** the concert ended. |
| after | answers the question *what happened next?* | We went home **after** the singer sang his first song. |
| although | tells you something is surprising | **Although** we did not really want to, we went home. |
| if | something needs to happen for something else to happen | **If** we get tired, we'll go home. |

## B Other connecting words

The words in this chart make connections between words and phrases

| Word | Function | Example |
| --- | --- | --- |
| only | says something is smaller or less than usual | He sleeps **only** three hours every night. |
| even | says something is surprising or unusual | Everyone was on time for the meeting, **even** Pat, who's usually late. |
| like | makes a comparison | She looks **like** her dad. |
| than | used after a comparative adjective or adverb | Ann is older **than** Chris. She works harder **than** he does. |
| too / also / as well | says something is in addition | He works in the store, and she does, **too**. He works in the store and **also** at home. |

# Exercises

**15.1** Circle one of the <u>underlined</u> words to complete these sentences.

1. Sam liked school (because) / although / if he had
   many friends there.
2. Sam graduated from school <u>if / but / and</u> got a job in a new city.
3. He made new friends, <u>but / before / after</u> he missed his
   friends from school.
4. <u>So / But / Before</u> Sam moved back to be near his school friends.
5. He was happy <u>because / although / and</u> he had no job.

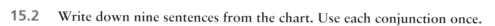

**15.2** Write down nine sentences from the chart. Use each conjunction once.

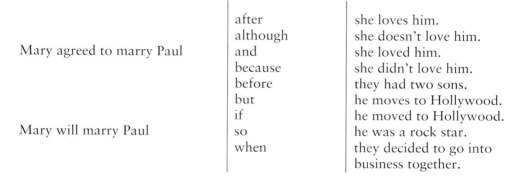

| | | |
|---|---|---|
| | after | she loves him. |
| | although | she doesn't love him. |
| Mary agreed to marry Paul | and | she loved him. |
| | because | she didn't love him. |
| | before | they had two sons. |
| | but | he moves to Hollywood. |
| | if | he moved to Hollywood. |
| Mary will marry Paul | so | he was a rock star. |
| | when | they decided to go into business together. |

**15.3** Fill in the blanks with words from B on page 30.

Pedro loves swimming, and his family loves swimming (1) .............................. . Everyone
in his family swims every day, (2) ............................. his grandmother! Pedro can swim
really well, but his father can swim better. Pedro's father swims (3) .............................
a fish. The father swims better (4) ............................. almost everyone. He learned to
swim when he was (5) ............................. two years old!

**15.4** Think about your family and your habits. Write sentences about your habits with
*only, even, than, like, also, too,* and *as well.* Now write a similar story about
you and your family.

*I play tennis and my mother plays, too. My mother plays better than my father.*

**15.5** Complete these sentences about yourself.

1. I am learning English because .................................................................................. .
2. I'll learn more English if .......................................................................................... .
3. I am learning English, and ....................................................................................... .
4. I am learning English, but ........................................................................................ .
5. I started learning English when ................................................................................ .
6. I can speak some English, so .................................................................................... .

# Time words

## A Basic time words

There are:

365 days in a year.
12 months in a year.
52 weeks in a year.
7 days in a week.

24 hours in a day.
60 minutes in an hour. (*Note*: **an** hour)
60 seconds in a minute.
100 years in a century.

## B Days of the week

**Sunday, Monday, Tuesday, Wednesday, Thursday, Friday, Saturday**

The names of the days always begin with a capital letter in English.
Saturday + Sunday = the **weekend** (in most English-speaking countries)

the day before ⟵ yesterday ⟵ today ⟶ tomorrow ⟶ the day after
yesterday                                                    tomorrow

Monday **morning** = Monday before 12 noon
Monday **afternoon** = Monday between 12 noon and about 5 or 6 p.m.
Monday **evening** = Monday from about 5 or 6 p.m. until 9 or 10 p.m.
We say **on** + days of the week: on Monday, on Saturday, etc.
    I saw her **on Friday / on Tuesday** evening.
We say **on/over** + the weekend.
    Is the market open **on the weekend / over the weekend**?

## C Months and seasons

Months: **January, February, March, April, May, June, July, August, September, October, November, December**

The names of the months always begin with a capital letter in English.

spring        summer        fall/autumn        winter

Some countries have four seasons: **spring, summer, fall** (**autumn**), and **winter**.

We say **in** + months/seasons: in **July**, in **May**, in (the) **fall**, in (the) **summer**, etc.
    My birthday is **in March**. (*not* ~~on~~ March) Birds sing **in** (**the**) **spring**.

---

*tip*   *Write the day and date in English whenever you do an English exercise.*

# Exercises

**16.1**   Complete these sentences with a word from A on page 32.

1. There are 3,600 seconds in .*an hour.*...........
2. There are 1,200 months in ......................... .
3. There are 168 hours in ......................... .
4. There are 8,760 hours in ......................... .

**16.2**   These abbreviations [short forms] are often used for the days of the week and the months of the year. Write out the names in full.

1. Mon.
2. Aug.
3. Oct.
4. Sat.
5. Wed.
6. Jan.
7. Apr.
8. Thurs.
9. Feb.
10. Sept.
11. Tues.
12. Nov.

**16.3**   Complete this table by putting each of the 12 months of the year in the box by the number of days in each month.

| Number of days in the month | Month |
|---|---|
| 30 | |
| 31 | December |
| 28/29 | |

**16.4**   What are the next few letters in each case? Explain why.

1. S   M   T   W   ?   ?   ?
2. J   F   M   A   M   J   J   ?   ?   ?   ?   ?

**16.5**   Correct the five mistakes in this paragraph.

I'm going to a party on saturday for Jill's birthday. Her birthday is on tuesday, but she wanted to have the party on the Weekend. She's having a barbecue. I think spring is a good time to have a party because of the weather. I love going to barbecues on the spring. My birthday is in Winter, and it's too cold to eat outside then!

**16.6**   Quiz: How quickly can you answer these questions?

1. What season is it now?
2. What day of the week is it today?
3. What day will it be the day after tomorrow?
4. What day was it the day before yesterday?
5. What is the seventh month of the year?
6. What month is it now?
7. What are the days of the week backwards starting with Sunday?
8. How many minutes are there in half an hour?
9. What month is your birthday in?
10. What part of the day is between morning and evening?

# Describing time: when

## A  Time in relation to now

**Now** means *at this moment*. **Then** means *at another moment* (in the past or in the future).

It is 10 **o'clock** now.
I got up **2 hours ago**, at 8 o'clock.
I'll eat lunch **in 2 hours**.
Then it will be **noon** / 12 o'clock.

**for two years** [for + a period of time]
**from 1997 to 1999**                1997 ⟶ 1999
I lived in Brazil **for two years**. I worked in Rio de Janeiro **from 1997 to 1999**.

**last year / last week / last Saturday**
**next year / next week / next summer**

Now it is July.
**Last** month was June.
**Next** month it will be August.

| JULY | | | | | | |
|---|---|---|---|---|---|---|
| SUN | MON | TUE | WED | THU | FRI | SAT |
| | | | 1 | 2 | 3 | 4 |
| 5 | 6 | 7 | 8 | 9 | 10 | 11 |
| 12 | 13 | 14 | 15 | 16 | 17 | 18 |
| 19 | 20 | 21 | 22 | 23 | 24 | 25 |
| 26 | 27 | 28 | 29 | 30 | 31 | |

When we talk about time in general, we talk about **the past, the present,** and **the future**.

> **In the past** people didn't have computers.
> People may travel to Mars **in the future**.
> Paulo will e-mail you **later**.
> I'll be with you **in a minute**. [a very short time in the future – not 60 seconds]
> I want you to do it **right now**. [at this very moment, not later]
> See you **soon**! [in a short time] We met **recently**. [not long ago]

## B  Frequency adverbs

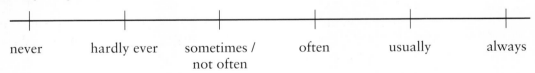

never        hardly ever        sometimes /        often        usually        always
                               not often

It **always** snows in Canada during the winter. It snows **every day** in the winter.
It **often** rains in Seattle. It rains **every week** in September.
The temperature in Tokyo **hardly ever** [almost never] gets to 100°F (38°C).
It **never** snows in Singapore.

Note the use of **a** in these expressions of frequency:
> **once** [one time] a week: I go swimming **once a week**, every Saturday.
> **twice** [two times] a day: I brush my teeth **twice a day**.
> **three** times a month: I play soccer **three or four times a month**.
> **four** times a year: I see my uncle **four times a year**.

# Exercises

**17.1**  Fill in the blanks with prepositions (e.g., *in, at, for*) from A on page 34.

(1) ...... *In* ........ the past, Rosa worked in many different countries. She worked in Hong Kong (2) ................. three years – (3) ................. 2005 (4) ................. 2008. (5) ................. the moment Rosa is working in Tokyo. She will stay there (6) ................. two more years.

**17.2**  Read these sentences and answer the questions.

1. Peter will get his test scores very soon. Do you think he will get them next year, next month, or tomorrow?
2. Sang Hee and Ali met for the first time recently. Do you think they first met last year, six months ago, or a week ago?
3. I'll help you in a minute. Do you think I'll help you next week, in two hours, or in a few minutes?

**17.3**  Are these sentences true about you? If not, write them out correctly. Use other frequency adverbs from B on page 34.

1. I always read e-mail in the morning.   *Sometimes I read e-mail in the morning.*
2. I usually take the bus to school/work.
3. I hardly ever play soccer.
4. Sometimes I watch TV on Saturday.
5. I hardly ever drink milk.
6. I often wear a hat.
7. Sometimes I eat chocolate.
8. I always go to bed at 10.
9. I never go to the movies.

**17.4**  Look at this table and make sentences using expressions like *once a week*, *twice a week*, *three times a month*.

Example: *Stefan practices the piano once a week.*

| | *Play tennis* | *Practice the piano* | *Have a business meeting in Toronto* |
|---|---|---|---|
| Stefan | Mondays and Thursdays | Saturdays | the first Friday of every month |
| Alicia and Amy | Tuesdays, Fridays, and Saturdays | every morning and every evening | once in January, March, May, July, August, and December every year |

**17.5**  Write a paragraph about your own life using as many of the words and expressions from page 34 as possible.

*I usually get up early. I always have a cup of coffee ...*

# Describing place: where

## A  General place words

Come **here** [to me, to where I am], please.
Have you ever been to Peru? I'm going **there** [to another place, not here] in May.
There are books and papers **everywhere** [in all parts / all places] in my room.
(See Unit 7 for the use of **come** and **go**.)

## B  Positions

the **top** of the mountain

the **middle** of the road

the **bottom** of the glass

the **front** of the car

the **side** of the car

the **back** of the car

the **beginning** of the book

the **end** of the book

## C  *Left* and *right*

his **right** hand

his **left** hand

## D  *Home* and *away*

Is Rachel **home / at home**? [in her house/apartment]
 No, she's **out**. [shopping / at work / at school]
 No, she's **away**. [in another town/city or country]
 No, she's **out of town**. [in another town/city]
Rachel is going **overseas** next year. [to another country]

# Exercises

**18.1**   **Match the expression on the left with the correct response on the right.**

1. I took my mother to Disneyland.
2. I take a book with me everywhere I go.
3. Is her room clean?
4. When did you come here to study?
5. My sister is coming over after class.
6. I went to Canada to study.

a. You must read a lot!
b. I came in August.
c. Why did you take her there?
d. No, there are clothes everywhere!
e. I went there to study, too!
f. What time will she get here?

**18.2**   **Mark these positions on the bus and on the tree.**

1. the front of the bus
2. the side of the bus
3. the back of the bus
4. the top of the tree
5. the bottom of the tree

**18.3**   **Fill in the blanks with *out*, *away*, *out of town*, or *overseas*.**

1. I'd like to work ......................... and learn about a new country.
2. Is Luis here? No, he's ......................... , but he'll be back in a minute.
3. I'm going ......................... tomorrow, to my sister's. She lives about 100 miles (160 kilometers) north of here.
4. When we go ......................... , we like to go ......................... and see new countries.

**18.4**   **Answer these questions about yourself and about this book.**

1. Are you studying English at home or overseas? *I'm studying English at home, in my country.*
2. Are you going away this year?

3. What do you have in your left or right hand at the moment?

4. Where is the unit on **Have** in this book? (beginning/middle/end?)

5. Where is the unit on **Feelings**? (beginning/middle/end?)

# Describing manner: how

Manner = **how** we do something or **the way** we do something.
We use adverbs to do this.

**A** *Fast / quickly* and *slowly*

She reads **fast/quickly**.
She's a **fast/quick** reader.

She reads very **slowly**.
She's a **slow** reader.

**B** *Loudly* and *quietly / softly*

He sings **loudly**. [His voice is loud.]
He is a **loud** singer.

She talks **quietly/softly**.
[It is difficult to hear her.]
She has a **quiet/soft** voice.

**C** *Well* and *badly / poorly*

She swims **well**.
She's a **good** swimmer.

He swims **badly/poorly**.
He's a **bad/poor** swimmer.

**D** *Right* and *wrong*

I like coffee a lot. ✓ ⟶ This sentence is **right**. [correct]
I like a lot coffee. ✗ ⟶ This sentence is **wrong**. [not correct]

# Exercises

**19.1** **Complete these sentences.**

1. This train is **slow**. It goes very ...*slowly*............
2. She is a **bad** writer. She writes very ......................... .
3. He is always **loud**. He speaks very ......................... .
4. This is a **fast** computer. It's very ......................... .
5. That little girl is **quiet**. She plays ......................... .
6. He's a **good** English speaker. He speaks English ......................... .

**19.2** **Which do you think is better? Use a dictionary if you need help.**

1. A loud person or a quiet person? *Usually a quiet person is better.* ............................
2. A fast bus or a slow bus? ...............................................................................
3. To speak loudly or speak softly? .....................................................................
4. A right answer or a wrong answer? ..................................................................
5. To work slowly or work quickly? ....................................................................
6. To sing well or sing poorly? ...........................................................................

**19.3** **Find six words from page 38.**

| | | | | |
|---|---|---|---|---|
| w | r | o | n g | b |
| e | c | i | g | l | a |
| l | u | b | b | a | d |
| l | o | u | d | h | l |
| s | f | a | s | t | y |

**19.4** **Use a dictionary to complete this chart. Write (✓) if the meaning is right, and (✗) if the meaning is wrong.**

| Word | Meaning | (✓) Right (✗) Wrong |
|---|---|---|
| suddenly | very slowly | ✗ |
| sadly | in an unhappy way | |
| strangely | not in a normal way | |
| safely | in a dangerous way | |
| easily | with no difficulty | |

**19.5** **Write at least five sentences about yourself and your friends/family. Use the words from page 38.**

*My sister plays tennis well. I sing badly.*

# Irregular verbs

Most English verbs are regular, like **play**. They form the past tense by adding -ed.

| **Base form** | | **Past tense** | | **Past participle** |
|---|---|---|---|---|
| play | ⟶ | play**ed** | ⟶ | play**ed** |
| I play tennis | | I played tennis | | I have played tennis |
|    every weekend. | |    yesterday. | |    for five years. |

But some common verbs in English are irregular (do not form the past tense by adding -ed).

| **Base form** | | **Past tense** | | **Past participle** |
|---|---|---|---|---|
| have | ⟶ | had | ⟶ | had |
| go | ⟶ | went | ⟶ | gone |
| get | ⟶ | got | ⟶ | gotten |

Below, the irregular verbs are grouped by how many forms change. When you learn a new irregular verb, add it to one of the groups of verbs on this page.

**A**   **All forms the same**

**cost, cut, hurt, let, put, shut,** and **read***
*The three forms of **read** are spelled the same but the past tense and past participle are not pronounced the same as the base form.

**B**   **Two different forms**

| First and third forms the same | | |
|---|---|---|
| become became become | come came come | run ran run |

| Second and third forms the same | | |
|---|---|---|
| bring brought brought | leave left left | sit sat sat |
| buy bought bought | lose lost lost | sleep slept slept |
| catch caught caught | make made made | spend spent spent |
| feel felt felt | meet met met | stand stood stood |
| fight fought fought | pay paid paid | teach taught taught |
| find found found | say said said | tell told told |
| have had had | sell sold sold | think thought thought |
| hear heard heard | send sent sent | understand understood understood |
| keep kept kept | shoot shot shot | win won won |

**C**   **Three different forms**

| | | |
|---|---|---|
| be was/were been | forget forgot forgotten | see saw seen |
| begin began begun | get got gotten | sing sang sung |
| break broke broken | give gave given | sink sank sunk |
| choose chose chosen | go went gone | speak spoke spoken |
| do did done | know knew known | steal stole stolen |
| drink drank drunk | ride rode ridden | swim swam swum |
| drive drove driven | ring rang rung | wake woke woken |
| eat ate eaten | take took taken | wear wore worn |
| fall fell fallen | tear tore torn | write wrote written |
| fly flew flown | throw threw thrown | |

# Exercises

**20.1** Complete this table using the verbs on page 40. Use a dictionary if you need help.

| Base form | Past tense | Past participle | Opposite |
|---|---|---|---|
| come | came | come | go |
| | | | lose |
| throw | | | |
| | | sat | |
| | began | | |
| | | | sell |

**20.2** Use the pictures to complete this story about Jane's day.
Use the correct past tense form.

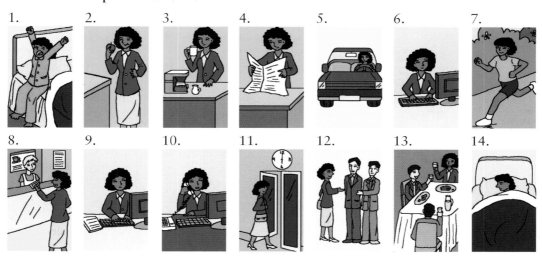

Yesterday Jane (1) ..*woke/got*.......... up at 7:00. She (2) ............................. an apple
and (3) ............................. a cup of coffee. She (4) ............................. the newspaper
and then (5) ............................. to work. At work she (6) ............................. some
e-mails. At lunch she (7) ............................. in the park for half an hour. Then she (8)
............................. a sandwich. After lunch she (9) ............................. at her desk and
(10) ............................. some phone calls. At 6:00 she (11) ............................. the
office and (12) ............................. some Japanese visitors. They (13) .............................
to a restaurant together. After her busy day Jane (14) ............................. very well.

**20.3** Complete the sentences with verbs from page 40. Use the correct past participle form.

1. Eric hasn't ..*seen*............... Julie since high school.
2. We haven't ......................... to Europe in years.
3. Have you ......................... lunch yet?
4. I have ......................... a lot of books this semester.
5. I've ......................... Celia for years. She's my best friend.
6. Have you ......................... the latest Batman movie?

# Common uncountable words

## A  What is countable and uncountable?

apples          shoes          plates

sugar          homework          baggage/luggage

**Countable**
Nouns you can count and make plural: **four apples, two shoes**

**Uncountable**
Nouns you can't count and can't make plural: not **three homeworks, four baggages**

Can I have **three apples** and **some sugar**, please?
**Are** these **shoes** yours?
**Is** this your **homework**?

## B  Everyday uncountable words

This **furniture**
is expensive.

You should ...

Let me give you
some **advice**.

This is hard **work**.

The **weather** is
terrible today.

You can get
**information** here.

There is a lot of
**traffic** today.

Air **travel** is fast.

There is some
bad **news** today.

I need some fresh **air**.

## C  Food

Many uncountable nouns are kinds of food and drink.

rice          spaghetti          butter          bread          beef          milk          water

*tip*  *When you learn a new noun, write it down in a phrase that shows if it is countable or uncountable.*

# Unit 21

## Exercises

### 21.1 Fill in the blanks with an uncountable noun from page 42.

1. I don't have any ...*homework*...... to do tonight.
2. Cows give us ........................ and ........................ .
3. My friend gave me some good ........................ about learning vocabulary.
4. There is always a lot of ........................ in the center of the city.
5. Somsak graduates next month and is looking for ........................ .

### 21.2 Write the nouns in the box in the correct column.

> cup   rice   traffic   book   pen   advice   information   train   news   work
> shirt   butter   teacher   milk   car   coffee   furniture   banana   money

| Countable nouns | Uncountable nouns |
|---|---|
| cup | |

### 21.3 Fill in the blanks with the correct form of the verb *be*.

1. Work ...*is/was*... the most important thing in Sam's life.
2. Their furniture ........................ very old and very beautiful.
3. Those chairs ........................ very expensive.
4. Last summer, the weather in Japan ........................ very bad.
5. The news ........................ better today than it ........................ yesterday.
6. How many apples ........................ in a pound (0.45 kilograms)?
7. Spaghetti with tomato sauce ........................ very good.
8. Air travel ........................ often tiring.

### 21.4 Correct the mistakes.

1. The news are not very good today. *The news is not very good today.*
2. I'd like some informations about your country.
3. Let me give you an advice.
4. Cook these rice for 30 minutes.
5. Maria is looking for a new work.
6. There's usually a better weather in the east than in the west.
7. We should buy some new furnitures.
8. I saw many traffic on my way to school.

# Adjectives describing good and bad things

**A** "Good" adjectives

a **good** hotel
three stars ***

a **better** hotel
four stars ****

the **best** hotel in town
five stars *****

This hotel is **better than** that one.

nice / beautiful / great / terrific / wonderful / excellent

A: That's a **nice** jacket.
B: Thank you.

A: It's a **beautiful** day today!
B: Yes, it is.

A: Do you want to go to the beach on Sunday?
B: That's a **great** idea / an **excellent** idea!
   [very, very good]

A: Have you been to the new mall?
B: Yes, the sales are **terrific**!

A: There's a **wonderful** park down the street.
B: **Great**, let's go!

When you answer and want to say how you feel:
A: We'll eat at 6:00 and then go to the movie afterwards.
B: **Great!/Terrific!/Perfect!**

**B** "Bad" adjectives

bad (worse / the worst) / awful / terrible

**bad** weather

My room looks **awful**!

Martina had a **bad** headache on Wednesday.
Today the weather is **worse than** yesterday.
That's the **worst** movie I've ever seen.
I had a **terrible** day at work today.

**C** That's + "good" and "bad" adjectives

A: I have to get up at 5:30 a.m. tomorrow.
B: That's **awful**!

A: I just passed my driver's test.
B: That's **great**!

# Exercises

**22.1** **Complete these sentences.**

1. My hair looks ...*awful*............................... I really need a haircut.
2. Today's weather is ......................................... yesterday. Let's go to the park.
3. The traffic is ......................................... in the city. Take the train.
4. That's a(n) ......................................... idea! Let's do it!
5. Three tests on the same day! That's .........................................!
6. What a ......................................... house! The beach is only 300 feet (91 meters) away!
7. This hotel is awful. It's ......................................... the one last night.

**22.2** **What can you say when someone says these things to you?**

1. Do you like my new jacket? *Yes, it's very nice.*
2. I have to get up at 4:30 tomorrow morning.
3. Let's go out for dinner tonight.
4. Is there a good Japanese restaurant in town?
5. What kind of person is your English teacher?
6. I lost my keys.

**22.3** **Match a description on the left with an expression on the right.**

1. blue sky, sunny, 72°F (22°C)
2. five stars (*****), very famous
3. 95 out of 100 on the test
4. dark skies, wind, rain
5. we can take a taxi.

a. wonderful news
b. awful weather
c. nice weather
d. an excellent idea
e. the best hotel in town

**22.4** **Use a dictionary to put these new adjectives into the *good* or *bad* column.**

awesome   nasty   fantastic   fine   mean   gorgeous   horrible   super

| Good | Bad |
|---|---|
| awesome | |

**22.5** **Look at the adjectives in 22.4. Think of two nouns to go with each adjective.**

*awesome news / an awesome movie*

# Adjectives describing people

## A Saying good things about people

**Nice** is the most common word used for people who we like / who are good.

Lara's very **nice**.
Richard's a **nice** man.

If you want to use words that are stronger than **nice**, you can use **great, terrific,** or **wonderful**.

Ron is a **wonderful** teacher. All the students love him. He's **terrific!**
But we don't say "Karla is very wonderful." We just say, "Karla is **wonderful**."

If someone is good to people or animals, you can use **kind**.

She is **kind**. She helps people.

**Other "good" things about people**

My friend Antonio is very **friendly**.
Marta's a **happy** person.
All my friends are **smart**. Some are very **intelligent**.

Pat is very **thoughtful**. [kind, thinks
    about the feelings of others]
He always brings his mother flowers.

Their son is very **well behaved**.
    [good, behaves well]

## B Saying bad things about people

Laura is **not very nice**.
Nancy has a **terrible** temper. [gets angry and is unkind]
Al can be **mean** [say unkind things] when he's angry.
My aunt is a **difficult** person. [not easy to please] She is never happy.
That waiter made a **stupid** mistake. I ordered coffee and he brought me milk! (**Stupid**
    is a very strong word.)
I don't like **selfish** people. [people who think only of themselves]
Sometimes my teenage son can be **childish**. [behaves like a child]

## C Prepositions

Jean was very nice/kind **to** me when I was in the hospital.
You were mean **to** me yesterday!
It was nice/thoughtful **of** you to remember my birthday.

# Exercises

**23.1**  **What do you think B said? Complete the sentences.**

*Let me carry your bags.*

1. A: Alan's very nice.
   B: He's more than nice, he's ........................ !
2. A: George wasn't very nice to you, was he?
   B: No, he was really ........................ !
3. A: Hank doesn't like to give things to other people.
   B: Yes, he seems ........................ .
4. A: Does your little brother do well at school?
   B: Yes, he's very ........................ .

**23.2**  **Put the letters of each word in the correct order.  Use them to complete the crossword puzzle.**

MATRS    FIRRTECI    LYENDIFR    DNIK    PPHAY

OOGD    FULDERNOW    PIDSTU    BLETERRI

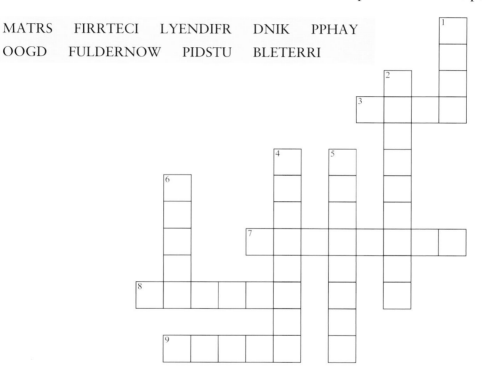

**23.3**  **Circle the words that describe you. Then use these words in sentences to describe yourself.**

friendly      sometimes difficult      terrific      kind to animals
sometimes stupid      nice to my friends      mean to some people
smart      selfish      intelligent      sometimes childish      thoughtful

**23.4**  **Fill in the blanks with the correct prepositions.**

1. The teacher is never mean ..........*to*.......... the students.
2. It is nice ........................ you to help me.
3. Pat is very kind ........................ everybody.
4. It was thoughtful ........................ him to call me.

# Unit 24

# Words and prepositions

### A Verb + preposition

I **listen to** music every morning.
I'll be a few minutes late. Please **wait for** me.
I **asked for** advice.
Where can I **pay for** this magazine?
The book **belongs to** me.

*I'm sorry I'm late.*

I'm **thinking about** the weekend.
Helena **thanked** her father **for** the present.
Jack **apologized for** being late.

### B Same verb, different preposition

Some verbs have different meanings when they are
used with different prepositions (e.g., **look**).

If you want to find something,
    (e.g., your key), you have to **look
    for** it.
If you don't know what a word means,
    you **look up** the word in a dictionary.
I love **looking at** old photographs.
You **look forward to** something good in the future (e.g., a trip or a party).

| look | |
|---|---|
| | for a key |
| | up a word |
| | at a book |
| | forward to a party |

### C Adjective + preposition

I'm **good at** science but **bad at** math.
I'm **interested in** sports.
He is **afraid of** mice.

### D Grammar

Prepositions are followed by a noun.
    Jo is good **at tennis.**

> *tip*    *When you read in English, write down phrases that use prepositions in a new way.*

48

# Exercises

**24.1** Match the phrases on the left with the phrases on the right to make sentences.

| | |
|---|---|
| 1. John is waiting | a. about his vacation. |
| 2. This umbrella belongs | b. for the money. |
| 3. Bill is thinking | c. for a bus. |
| 4. She apologized | d. for advice. |
| 5. Let me pay | e. to the hotel. |
| 6. They thanked their grandmother | f. for her mistake. |
| 7. Sandy asked her teacher | g. for our tickets. |

**24.2** Match the words in the box with the *look* expressions below. Some words go with more than one expression.

| keys | a word | dinner | glasses | pictures | the movie |
|---|---|---|---|---|---|
| an e-mail address | | the party | a phone number | | a vacation |

1. look for ...*keys*.....................................................................................
2. look up ....................................................................................................
3. look forward to ....................................................................................
4. look at ....................................................................................................

**24.3** Answer these questions about yourself.

1. What subjects were you good at in school? What subjects were you bad at?
   ..............................................................................................................
2. What sports are you good at?
   ..............................................................................................................
3. What or who are you proud of?
   ..............................................................................................................
4. What are you afraid of?
   ..............................................................................................................
5. What kind of music do you listen to?
   ..............................................................................................................
6. What are you looking forward to?
   ..............................................................................................................
7. What are you interested in?
   ..............................................................................................................

Prefixes come at the beginning of words. They can help you understand what a new word means.

**A** **Prefixes meaning *not***

Many prefixes can be added to words to make them negative.

| Prefix | Meaning | Examples |
| --- | --- | --- |
| in-, im- | not | informal, impossible |
| mis- | wrong or badly | misunderstand, misbehave |
| non- | not | nonsmoking, nonresident |
| un- | not | unhappy, unsafe |

**Informal** clothes are jeans and a T-shirt; **informal** language
   is phrases like "Hey! What's up?"
If something is **impossible**, you can't do it.
   It is **impossible** to read with your eyes closed.
If you **misunderstand** something (or someone), you think you
   understand or know it, but you really don't.
If someone **misbehaves**, then he or she is behaving badly.
A **nonsmoking** room is a room where people cannot smoke.
A **nonresident** is someone who has his or her home somewhere else.

**informal**   **formal**

**B** **Other prefixes**

Here are some other common prefixes.

| Prefix | Meaning | Examples |
| --- | --- | --- |
| ex- | was, but not now | ex-wife, ex-boss |
| pre- | before | preschool |
| re- | again | redo, rewrite |

An **ex-wife** is a wife who is now divorced from her husband.
An **ex-boss** is someone you no longer work for.
A **preschool** is a school for children who are too young to go to regular school.
To **redo** something is to do it again.
To **rewrite** something is to write it again.

 *tip*    *Sometimes words with prefixes have a hyphen (-) (e.g., ex-wife), and sometimes they don't (e.g., impossible). Use a dictionary when you are not sure if there is a hyphen.*

# Exercises

**25.1** **Complete the sentences with words from page 50.**

1. Sarah is too young for regular school. She goes to ..*preschool.*...............
2. I can't read this. Please .................................... your homework.
3. We often say "What's up?" in .................................... English.
4. I liked school, but my sister was very .................................... there.
5. Those children cause a lot of trouble. They .................................... all the time.
6. Don't walk on that sidewalk. The sign says it is .................................... .

**25.2** **What do you think these words and phrases mean? Look at the charts on page 50 to help you.**

1. an ex-husband *a husband now divorced from his wife* ................
2. pre-cooked rice ......................................................................
3. an incorrect answer ...............................................................
4. to reread a book ....................................................................
5. to retell a story ....................................................................
6. a misspelled word .................................................................
7. an unfinished e-mail ..............................................................
8. a nonsmoking section ............................................................
9. an ex-boyfriend ....................................................................
10. an impossible task ...............................................................

**25.3** **Match the prefixes on the left to the words on right. Then write a phrase or sentence using your word. Use a dictionary to help you.**

1. pre          a. fat
2. in           b. answered
3. re           c. judge
4. mis         d. paid
5. non        e. complete
6. un         f. paint

1. *I have prepaid tickets to the show tomorrow.* ................
2. ........................................................................................
3. ........................................................................................
4. ........................................................................................
5. ........................................................................................
6. ........................................................................................

**25.4** **Find the negative forms of these words. Use a dictionary if you need help.**

1. possible ..*impossible*..........................
2. comfortable ......................................
3. friendly..............................................
4. convenient ........................................
5. considerate ......................................
6. sure .................................................
7. polite ...............................................
8. correct .............................................

# Suffixes

Suffixes come at the end of words. They can help you understand the meaning of a new word.

**A** Noun suffixes

The suffixes **-er** or **-or** are added to verbs to mean a person or thing that does something.

> She swims every day. She is a good swimm**er**.
> He staples the pages together with a stapl**er**.
> He instructed her to hit the tennis ball harder. He is a good tennis instruct**or**.
> I calculate prices with a calculat**or** when I shop.

The suffixes **-ics** and **-ology** mean a subject of study.

> Econom**ics** is the study of money and finance.
> Polit**ics** is the study of governments.
> Studying psych**ology** teaches you about people.
> Studying soci**ology** teaches you about society.

The suffix **-ness** makes an adjective into a noun.

> The song filled her with happi**ness**.
> They said goodbye with great sad**ness**.

**B** Adjective suffixes

The suffixes **-y**, **-ful**, and **-less** make an adjective from a noun.

> That beach is long and sand**y**.
> It's a beautiful, sunn**y** day. Let's go to the beach!

The suffix **-ful** means *a lot of*.

> Thanks, the information was very use**ful**.
> What a beauti**ful** picture of a rose.

The suffix **-less** means *not a lot of*.

> This book is no help at all. It's use**less**.
> This book is end**less**. I can't finish it.

**C** Adverb suffixes

The suffix **-ly** makes an adverb from an adjective.

> He was late, so he walked quick**ly** to the train station.
> The child ran happi**ly** across the grass.

# Exercises

**26.1** Which words from A on page 52 do these pictures illustrate?

1. _economics_ ............................ 3. a s ................................. 5. a c................................

2. a golf i .......................... 4. a s ............................... 6. shows ..........................

**26.2** Match the books on the left with the subjects on the right.

1. *The President and Congress in the U.S.*        a. sociology
2. *South Korean Society Today*        b. mathematics
3. *The Future of Banking*        c. psychology
4. *Why People Smile*        d. economics
5. *Calculations in Computer Science*        e. politics

**26.3** Match the adjectives with the nouns in the box. Some adjectives go with more than one noun.

| beach | weather | car | idea | book | smile | picture |

1. beautiful    2. sunny    3. useful    4. useless    5. sandy    6. endless

*beautiful beach / weather / smile / picture*

**26.4** What do you think these words and phrases mean? Use the information about suffixes on page 52 to help you.

1. biology   *the study of life*
2. loneliness
3. slowly
4. hopeful
5. rainy
6. painless
7. badly
8. a can opener
9. cloudy
10. a surfer

### A  Every day

Good morning.

Good afternoon.

Good evening.

Hello.

Hi.

How are you?

Fine, thanks. How are you?

Pretty good.

When you leave someone, usually you both say **Goodbye** or maybe **See you later** or **Take care!** (informal)  If it's daytime, you can also say **Have a nice day!**

When someone goes to bed, you usually say **Good night**. You can also say **Sleep well**. Don't say **Good night** when you arrive somewhere, only when you leave at night.

If you ask for something, you often say **Please**.

If someone does something nice for you, say **Thank you** or **Thanks**. Then they say **You're welcome!**

If someone sneezes, you often say **Bless you**.

Bless you.

### B  Excuse me / sorry

Say **Excuse me** if you want to get someone's attention, didn't understand what they said, or need to walk through a group or line of people.

Say **Sorry** if you hear bad news, break something, or touch someone by mistake.

Excuse me!

Sorry!

### C  Special days

If someone is going to do something difficult (e.g., take a test or have a job interview), say **Good luck!**

If someone has done something special (e.g., done well on a test, gotten a new job, had a baby), say **Congratulations!**

When it is someone's birthday, say **Happy Birthday!** (*not* ~~Congratulations!~~)

On (or just after) January 1 (New Year's Day), say **Happy New Year!**

# Exercises

**27.1** Choose phrases from page 54 to fit the conversations.

1. A: *(sneezes)* Atchoo!
   B: *Bless you.* ...............................
2. A: I'm taking a math test today.
   B: ...............................
3. A: I passed my driving test!
   B: ...............................
4. A: Goodbye.
   B: ...............................
5. A: It's my birthday today.
   B: ...............................
6. A: Thank you.
   B: ...............................
7. A: Hello!
   B: ...............................
8. A: Here's your coffee.
   B: ...............................

**27.2** What is the person saying in each picture?

1.
2.
3.
4.
5.
6.

**27.3** What do you say? Choose a phrase from page 54.

1. You want to order a sandwich. The waiter is reading the newspaper.
   *Excuse me.*
2. A child says "Good night" to you.
3. You answer the phone at work. It is 10:30 a.m.
4. Your friend says her grandmother is in the hospital.
5. It is 2 a.m. on January 1. You meet a friend on the street.
6. A friend spoke too quickly. You didn't understand.

**27.4** Put these sentences in the correct order and read the conversations.

ANN: Fine, thanks. Today's my birthday.
ANN: Hi!
BILL: Happy Birthday!
BILL: Hi, how are you?

MICHAEL: Yes, please.
TOMOKO: Do you want something to drink?
MICHAEL: Thanks!
TOMOKO: Would you like lemonade? I just made some.

**27.5** Write a conversation using phrases from page 54. Use as many as possible.

# Unit 28

## Words and phrases you may confuse

**A** Pronouns

*its / it's*

Use **its** for something that belongs to a place or a thing.
   The school has **its** own swimming pool.

Use **it's** as a shortened form of *it is* or *it has*.
   My computer isn't very good. **It's** [it is] very slow.
   **It's** [it has] been raining all day.

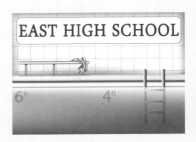

*their / they're*

Use **their** for something that belongs to them.
   The students were happy with **their** grades. They thanked **their** teacher.

Use **they're** as a shortened form of *they are*.
   **They're** [they are] going to be late for school.

*your / you're*

Use **your** for something that belongs to
someone you are talking to.
   I like **your** new coat!
Use **you're** as a shortened form of *you are*.
   **You're** [you are] good at basketball.

**B** Verbs

*watch / look at*

You **watch** something that's moving.
   Yolanda **watched** the soccer game.
You **look at** something that's not moving.
   I like to **look at** pictures of my family.

*look / see / listen / hear*

If you **look** at or **listen** to something, you are trying to see it or hear it.
   Olga **looked** at the test questions and **listened** carefully to the directions.
If you **see** or **hear** something, you are not trying to see or hear it.
   I **saw** a car drive by and **heard** a crash.

**C** Phrases often mixed up

*be used to / used to*

You **are used to** what you always do. [You feel comfortable doing it
because you do it often.] You have to **get used to** something new.
   **I'm used to** the traffic downtown.
   **I'm used to** getting up early. (*not* I'm used to ~~get~~ up)
   I have to **get used to** my new schedule.

Use **used to** to talk about things you did in the past, but not anymore.
   I **used to** play baseball, but then I hurt my arm.

# Exercises

**28.1** Complete these sentences with words from A on page 56.

1. The dog was chasing i ......................... tail.
2. Y ......................... learning a lot of new vocabulary.
3. They bought t ......................... concert tickets on the Internet.
4. I ......................... raining in New Delhi today.
5. T ......................... getting married next month.
6. Take y ......................... coat. It's going to be cold today.

**28.2** Match the verbs on the left with the nouns on the right.

1. watch           a. a bedtime story
2. hear            b. a street sign
3. see             c. a fire alarm
4. look at         d. TV
5. listen to       e. a painting

**28.3** Jimmy White worked very hard to become a wealthy businessman. Look at the
pictures, showing scenes from his life. Complete the sentences for each picture using *be
used to* or *used to*. Circle the correct verb.

1. He ..*'s used to*.........
   fly /(flying) first class.

3. He .............................
   sell / selling newspapers.

5. He .............................
   drive / driving nice cars.

2. He .............................
   live / living in a
   small apartment.

4. He .............................
   eat / eating in the best
   restaurants in town.

6. He .............................
   work / working for
   someone else.

**28.4** Complete this table with things you *used to* do and *are used to* doing now.

| I used to do this. | I'm used to doing this. |
|---|---|
|  |  |
|  |  |
|  |  |

# Birth, marriage, and death

### A Birth

Diana **had a baby** boy yesterday.
He **was born** at 1:15 in the morning on June 16.

She **named** him Benjamin **after** his grandfather.
    (His grandfather's name is Benjamin, too.)
His grandfather's **birthday** is June 16, too –
    but he **was born** in 1958!
The baby's parents **were born** in 1985.

### B Marriage

If you have a husband or wife, you are **married**.
If you are not married, you are **single**.
If her husband dies, a woman is a **widow**. If his wife dies, a man is a **widower**.
If your marriage legally ends, you are **divorced**.

**The wedding**

Javier and Claudia **got married**.
Claudia **married** Javier. (*not* ~~with~~
    Javier)
They went to Hawaii on their
    **honeymoon**.
They **were married** for 20 years.

bride (bride)groom

### C Death

Javier **died** last year. (*not* Javier ~~is~~ died)
His **death** was very sad and unexpected.
He **died of** a heart attack.
Javier is **dead**.
Now Claudia is a **widow**.

the funeral

## Exercises

**29.1** **When were these people *born* and when did they *die*? Write sentences.**

**Elvis Presley (1935–1977)**

1. Christopher Columbus (1451–1506)
   *Christopher Columbus was born in 1451. He died in 1506.*
2. Mother Teresa (1910–1997)
3. Benjamin Franklin (1706–1790)
4. Elvis Presley (1935–1977)
5. Leonardo da Vinci (1452–1519)
6. Martin Luther King, Jr. (1929–1968)

**29.2** **Fill in the blanks with *died*, *dead*, or *death*.**

1. Jill's grandfather ......................... last year.
2. His ......................... was a great shock to her.
3. Her grandmother has been ......................... for five years now.
4. She ......................... of a heart attack.
5. Now all of Jill's grandparents are ......................... .

**29.3** **Find a word or phrase on page 58 to match these descriptions.**

1. a woman on her wedding day *a bride*
2. a man on his wedding day
3. what you are if you have never been married
4. a person who is four months old
5. what you are if your marriage has legally ended
6. a ceremony, usually religious, after a person dies
7. a vacation after a wedding
8. what you are if your husband dies

**29.4** **Fill in the blanks with words from the box.**

| named | honeymoon | birthday | died | born | married | death | wedding |

In 1997, Anne (1) ......................... Robert Smith. Unfortunately, Robert's grandmother, Rose, (2) ......................... soon after their (3) ......................... . Robert and Anne were on their (4) ......................... at the time of her (5) ......................... . Their baby daughter was (6) ......................... two years later. They (7) ......................... the baby Rose, after Robert's grandmother. The baby has the same (8) ......................... as her father.

**29.5** **Write about your family. Use words and expressions from page 58. Write at least five sentences.**

*My mother was born in Buenos Aires on July 4, 1955.*

# The family

**A**  Here is a **family tree** [a drawing that shows all the members of a family] for some of Paul Mason's **relatives**. [people in their family]

Henry and Diana are Paul's **parents**.
Paul is their **son**.
Carol is Paul's **sister**. John and George are Paul's **brothers**.
Anne is Paul's **wife** and Sarah's **mother**.
Paul is Anne's husband and Sarah's **father**.
Anne and Paul are Sarah's **parents**.
Sarah is Anne and Paul's **daughter**.

Paul's brothers, John and George, are Sarah's **uncles**.
Paul's sister, Carol, is Sarah's **aunt**.
Sarah is Carol, John, George, and Sandra's **niece**.
Emily is Paul's **niece**.
Peter is his **nephew**.
Emily and Peter are Sarah's **cousins**.

Henry is Sarah's **grandfather**. Diana is her **grandmother**.
Henry and Diana are Sarah's **grandparents**.
Sarah and Emily are Henry and Diana's **granddaughters**.
Peter is Henry and Diana's **grandson**.

# Exercises

**30.1**  Look at the family tree on page 60. Complete the sentences.

1. Emily is Peter's ..*sister*...........
2. Peter is Emily's ........................ .
3. Anne is Emily's ........................ .
4. Paul is Peter's ........................ .
5. Diana is Peter's ........................ .
6. Henry is Emily's ........................ .
7. Peter is Paul's ........................ .
8. Emily is Paul's ........................ .
9. Sandra is Emily's ........................ .
10. Sandra is George's ........................ .
11. Sarah is Peter's ........................ .
12. Peter is Henry and Diana's ........................ .

**30.2**  Draw your family tree. Then write about your relatives.

*I am Tony. Anne is my wife.*

**30.3**  Match the descriptions on the left with the correct words on the right.

1. Your parent's parents are your
2. Your father or mother's brothers are your
3. The children of your mother or father's brothers/sisters are your
4. Your mother's husband is your
5. Your father's sister is your

   a. uncles.
   b. cousins.
   c. father.
   d. aunt.
   e. grandparents.

**30.4**  Ask a friend these questions. Then write sentences about your friend's family.

1. Do you have any brothers and sisters?
   *Chen has one brother and no sisters.*
2. Do you have any cousins?
   .......................................................................
3. Do you have any nieces or nephews?
   .......................................................................
4. Do you have any grandparents?
   .......................................................................
5. Do you have any aunts or uncles?
   .......................................................................

# Unit 31

## Parts of the body

**A**  Head and face

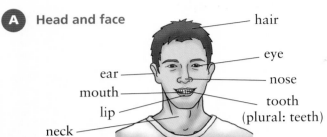

- hair
- eye
- ear
- nose
- mouth
- tooth (plural: teeth)
- lip
- neck

**B**  Arm and leg

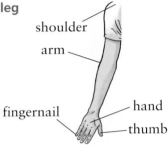

- shoulder
- arm
- fingernail
- hand
- thumb

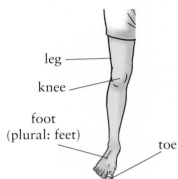

- leg
- knee
- foot (plural: feet)
- toe

**C**  Rest of the body

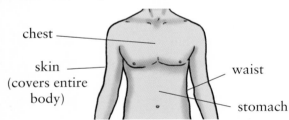

- chest
- skin (covers entire body)
- waist
- stomach

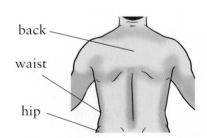

- back
- waist
- hip

**D**  Inside the body

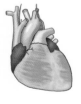

heart

brain

blood

**E**  Grammar

Use *my*, *your*, *his*, *her*, etc., with parts of the body (usually).
    Jane is washing **her** hair. (*not* Jane is washing ~~the~~ hair.)
    I have a pain in **my** leg. (*not* I have a pain in ~~the~~ leg.)

## Exercises

**31.1** Complete these sentences with words from page 62.

1. A hand has five ........*fingers.*........
2. You put shoes on your ......................... .
3. You see with your ......................... .
4. You smell with your ......................... .
5. A foot has five ......................... .
6. You hear with your ......................... .
7. You use your ......................... to think!
8. Your ......................... type can be A, B, AB, or O.
9. You run with your ......................... .
10. Your eyes, nose, and mouth are part of your ......................... .

**31.2** Parts of the body are often used in compound nouns [two nouns joined together to make a new noun, e.g., *schoolteacher* = *school* + *teacher*]. Complete these nouns with a word from page 62.

1. ..........*arm* chair

3. ...................... stick

5. ...................... rings

2. ...................... ball

4. ...................... brush

6. ...................... pack

**31.3** Cover page 62. Label the parts of the body.

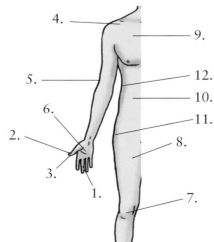

## A  Types of clothes

coat    jacket    scarf    gloves    shoes    boots    suit    hat

socks    T-shirt    shirt    dress    skirt    (neck)tie    belt    sweater

My **suit** is new.

## B  Plural words

These words are always plural in English. They need a plural verb.

pants    jeans    shorts    glasses    sunglasses

These **pants are** old. Her **shorts/jeans are** black.

> *tip*    *You can also say a pair of shorts / (sun)glasses / pants / jeans.*

## C  Verbs

You **wear** clothes. (*not* you ~~use~~ clothes)
You **carry** things.

Sue **is wearing** a long red coat. She has a suitcase, and she's carrying a small purse. Yesterday, she **wore** a blue coat, and she **carried** an umbrella and a briefcase.

You can also say: Sue **has** a red coat **on**.
Yesterday, she **had** a blue coat **on**.

In the morning you **get dressed** or **put on** your clothes.
At night you **get undressed** or **take off** your clothes.

> *tip*    *Write down the name for all the clothes you usually wear. Use a dictionary if you need help.*

# Exercises

**32.1**  Unscramble these words.

1. tirsk …*skirt*………………………………
2. jekcat ………………………………………
3. soskc ………………………………………
4. tebl ………………………………………
5. weerast ……………………………………

6. acrfs ………………………………………
7. trish ………………………………………
8. tius ………………………………………
9. storsh ………………………………………
10. mlrueabl ……………………………………

**32.2**  Match the part of the body with the item of clothing.

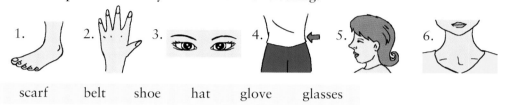

scarf    belt    shoe    hat    glove    glasses

**32.3**  Choose a verb from the box and put it in the correct form. Verbs may be used more than once.

| be | wear | carry | put | get dressed | have | take |
|----|------|-------|-----|-------------|------|------|

1. John's jeans ………*are*……… blue, and his T-shirt ……………………… red.
2. Julia …………………… jeans and a T-shirt yesterday.
3. It was cold outside, so Mai …………………… on a coat. She …………………… off her coat when she got to school.
4. At the party Sarah …………………… a red dress on, and she …………………… some flowers.
5. Siree's shirt …………………… old, but her shoes …………………… new.
6. Yesterday Antonio's pants …………………… white. Today they …………………… gray.
7. …………………………… this a new pair of jeans?
8. In the morning after you wake up you ……………………………… .

**32.4**  Look at the picture and write the name of the item of clothing next to the number.

1. *sunglasses*………
2. ……………………
3. ……………………
4. ……………………
5. ……………………
6. ……………………
7. ……………………
8. ……………………
9. ……………………
10. ……………………
11. ……………………

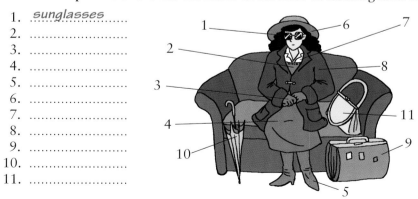

**32.5**  Write a paragraph about what you are wearing today.

*I'm wearing a white T-shirt and a blue sweater. I have a pair of black pants on. I'm wearing blue socks and white shoes. I also have a pair of glasses on.*

# Describing people's appearance

### A Height [How many feet and inches or how many centimeters?]

Kate is a very **tall** woman. (*not* Kate is a very ~~high~~ woman.) Tom is **short**. (*not* Tom is ~~low~~.)
If you aren't tall or short, you are **average height**.
To ask if someone is tall or short, you say:
**How tall** is Kate/Tom?
She's **5 foot 10 / 5 10** [5 feet and 10 inches tall] (*not* 5 ~~feet~~ 10) / 178 centimeters.
He's **5 feet tall** / 152 centimeters. (*not* 5 ~~foot~~ tall)

Tom

Kate

### B Weight [How many pounds or kilos?]

Mee-sun is **slim**.
I was very **thin** when I was in the hospital. (**Thin** is a more negative word.)
I don't want to get **fat**. (**Fat** is a negative word.)
A **large** man opened the door. (more polite than fat)

Mee-sun

The doctor said I am **overweight**. [more pounds/kilos than is good for me]

**How much do you weigh?**
I weigh 154 pounds / 70 kilos.

### C Coloring

Sally has **dark** hair and **dark** skin.
She has **brown** eyes.
Liz has **blonde** hair and **light/fair** skin.
She has **blue** eyes.
Bill has a **beard**, a **mustache,** and **long** hair.
He has **green** eyes.
Taka has **short black** hair.

Sally          Liz

Bill          Taka

### D Age

My great-grandmother is 97. She's very **old**. My sister is 14. She's **young** but would like to be **older**. My father is 50. He's **middle-aged** but would like to be **younger!**

This nursing home is for **elderly** people. (more polite than old)

### E Looks

My sister is very **pretty**. (usually girls/women only)
She's a **beautiful** girl.
Jim's a very **handsome** man. (usually for boys/men only)
Bob is **unattractive/ugly**. (**ugly** is a very negative word)
I'm not ugly or beautiful. I'm just **average/ordinary-looking**.

# Exercises

**33.1**  **Fill in the blanks with words from page 66.**

1. He's only 4 foot 11 (150 centimeters). He's kind of *short.*
2. Very ............................................... people are often good at basketball.
3. Models are usually ............................................... .
4. Her skin isn't dark, it's ............................................... .
5. She's only six years old. She's very ............................................... .
6. If I eat too much, I'll get ............................................... .
7. My grandmother lives in a home for ............................................... people.
   (Don't use "old.")

**33.2**  **Ask questions for these answers. Use the words in parentheses.**

1. How *tall is Mitsu* ............................................... ? (Mitsu)
   He's about 5 foot 9 (175 centimeters).
2. Is ............................................... ? (Elena's hair)
   No, her hair's dark.
3. What ............................................... ? (Mike's eyes)
   They're blue.
4. Are ............................................... ? (your parents)
   Not really, they're middle-aged.
5. How ............................................... ? (Hiromi)
   She weighs 114 pounds (51.7 kilograms).

**33.3**  **Write sentences describing the people in these pictures.**

| Sue | Jeff | Wendy | Dick |

1. Sue has ............................................... .
2. Jeff has ............................................... .
3. Wendy has ............................................... .
4. Dick's hair is ......................................, and he ............................................... .

**33.4**  **Write down the names of three people you know and describe them. Write about these things.**

– their height (tall, short, average)
– their hair (color, long, short, beard)
– their eyes (color)
– their looks (average, handsome, etc.)

# Unit 34

# Sickness and health

### A How are you feeling?

Much **better**, thank you.   *or*   **Fine**, thanks.

I **don't feel very good.** I have to go home and rest.
I'll probably be OK tomorrow. (not a serious problem)

**I'm sick.** Can you call a doctor? (possibly a serious problem)

That fish was bad. I think I'm going to **vomit!** [throw up]

### B Everyday problems

**I have a headache.** Do you have any **aspirin**?

**I have a toothache.** I need to go to the **dentist**.

**I have a bad cough.**  Do you have any **cough syrup**?

**I have a cold.** I'm going to bed after I drink some hot tea. (See Unit 3 for expressions
with **have**.)

### C Problems people have for many years / all their lives

I get **allergies** every spring from
flowers and grass. I **sneeze** all day.

My little brother has **asthma**.
Sometimes he can't breathe.

sneeze

### D Serious illnesses

My father **had a heart attack**.
He is **in the hospital**.

Every year **cancer** kills many
people who smoke.

### E How to stay fit and healthy

Have a good **diet**: Eat lots of fruit and vegetables.
**Get some exercise**: Swimming, jogging, and cycling are good for you.
Don't have too much **stress**: Relax after work or class.
Don't worry about work!

68

# Exercises

**34.1**  Write these words in the correct column. Do you think these health problems are *not very serious, somewhat serious,* or *very serious*?

| a headache | cancer | a toothache | allergies | a cough |
|---|---|---|---|---|
| a heart attack | a cold | asthma | vomiting | |

| Not very serious | Somewhat serious | Very serious |
|---|---|---|
| a headache | | |

**34.2**  Complete the conversations.

1. A: How are you today?
   B: ...................................................................................................................
   A: Good!
2. A: Are you OK?
   B: No, ................................................................................................... .
   A: Do you want a glass of water?
   B: Yes, thank you.
3. A: I ................................................................................................................ .
   B: Should I call a doctor?
   A: Yes, I think so.
4. A: ...................................................................................................................
   B: Here's the phone number of a good dentist.
   A: Thanks.
5. A: You have a cough. Do you have ................................................................. .
   B: Yes.
   A: Why don't you have a hot drink and go to bed early?

**34.3**  What illnesses are connected with these things?

1. pollution, traffic fumes   *asthma*
2. too much stress
3. grass, flowers
4. smoking

**34.4**  Answer these questions about yourself.
Use a dictionary if you need help.

1. What do you think is a good diet?
2. What kind of exercise do you like?
3. Do you have a lot of stress in your life?
4. Have you ever been in the hospital?

# Feelings

## A Love / Like / Hate

love      like      don't like (dislike)      hate

**I love** my family and my best friend.
**I like** my job.
**I don't like** horror movies. ("**I dislike** horror movies" is less common.)
**I hate** traffic jams.

## B Want / Hope

**I want** [I would like] **a new car.** (**want** + noun)
**I want to buy** a new car. (**want** + infinitive)
Note: **I want my father to buy** a new car. (**want** + object + infinitive)
(*not* ~~I want that~~ . . .)
**I hope to get** an A on my test. (**hope** + infinitive)
**I hope** (**that**) my friend does well on his test. (**hope** + *that clause*)

## C Happy / Sad / Tired

sad

upset

angry

happy

hungry

surprised

tired

sick

thirsty

warm

cold

hot

# Exercises

**35.1** Do you *love, like, not like,* or *hate* these things? Write sentences.

1. coffee *..I hate coffee. I like tea.*............
2. cooking ...............................................
3. driving ...............................................
4. chocolate ...........................................

5. soccer ...............................................
6. cats ...................................................
7. dancing ..............................................
8. jazz ....................................................

**35.2** Answer these questions using *want* or *hope*.

1. You're thirsty. What do you want? *I want something to drink. / I want a drink.*
2. The class feels very long. What do you hope?
3. You're hungry. What do you want?
4. Your friend is sick. What do you hope?
5. You're tired. What do you want?
6. You haven't seen your best friend in months. What do you hope?

**35.3** Look at the pictures. How do these people feel? Use words from C on page 70.

1. Marie *...is hungry.*...........................

4. Bob ..................................................... .

2. Fred ..................................................... .

5. Mr. Lee ................................................ .

3. The children .................................... .

6. Mrs. Jones ..................................... .

**35.4** Write about a recent time when you felt these ways.

1. upset     2. surprised     3. angry     4. sad

*I felt upset this morning when I was late for work.*

# Unit 36

## Countries, languages, and people

All the nouns and adjectives in this unit always begin with a capital letter, e.g., Africa (*not* africa) and Spanish (*not* spanish).

### A  Continents and countries

The names of the continents are marked in blue. It is not possible to show all the countries of the world on this page. If your country is not included, check its English name with your teacher or in a reference book such as an atlas.

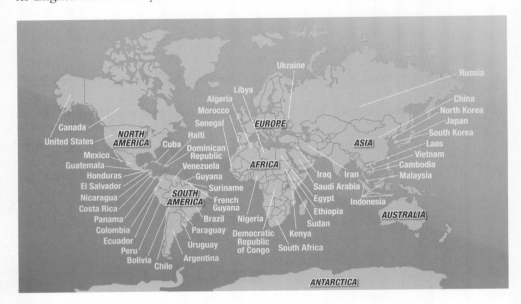

### B  People

Adjectives of nationality describe people and things from different countries, groups, or regions (e.g., a Brazilian man, a Korean woman, a Mexican family).

With **-an** or **-ian**:  Australian, Brazilian, Canadian, Chilean, Egyptian, Indonesian, Italian, Mexican, Peruvian, Russian, Venezuelan

With **-ish**:  British, Danish, Irish, Polish, Spanish, Swedish, Turkish

With **-ese**:  Chinese, Japanese, Portuguese, Senegalese, Vietnamese

Exceptions:  Dutch (from Holland), Filipino (from the Philippines), French (from France), Greek (from Greece), Iraqi (from Iraq), Swiss (from Switzerland), Thai (from Thailand)

### C  Languages and people

Words for languages are usually the same as the adjective of nationality: **Chinese, French, Japanese, Korean, Portuguese, Spanish, Thai,** etc. However, Arabs speak **Arabic**.

# Exercises

You may need to use a reference book to help you with some of these exercises.
It is not possible to include every country and nationality on page 72.

**36.1** **Name the continents where you find these places.**

1. Mount Everest *Asia*
2. the Alps
3. the Amazon River
4. the Great Barrier Reef
5. the Great Wall
6. the Andes Mountains
7. the Nile River
8. Mount Fuji
9. the Grand Canyon

**36.2** **Match these capital cities on the left with their countries on the right.**

1. Tokyo
2. Beijing
3. Seoul
4. Bogotá
5. Caracas
6. Washington, D.C.
7. Bangkok
8. Buenos Aires
9. Rome
10. Mexico City

a. Thailand
b. Italy
c. Mexico
d. China
e. Japan
f. Argentina
g. South Korea
h. Colombia
i. the United States
j. Venezuela

**36.3** **Answer these questions. Be sure to use the English terms.**

1. What is the name of your country?
2. What are the names of the countries next to your country?
3. What is the word for your language?
4. What are people from your country called?
5. In which continent is your country?

**36.4** **What is the adjective for people or things from these countries?**

1. Cuba *Cuban*
2. Thailand
3. Brazil
4. Canada
5. Mexico
6. the Philippines
7. France
8. Peru
9. China
10. Vietnam
11. Indonesia
12. Chile

**36.5** **Which country is different below? Think of the languages they speak there. Write sentences.**

1. England, Canada, Russia, Australia *In England, Canada, and Australia they speak English, but in Russia they speak Russian.*
2. Mexico, Brazil, Spain, Panama

3. Italy, Austria, Germany, Switzerland

4. Egypt, Saudi Arabia, Algeria, South Africa

# Unit 37    Weather

**A**  Types of weather

sun · rain · clouds · snow · fog · wind · thunder · lightning

**B**  Nouns, adjectives, and verbs

| Noun | Adjective |
|------|-----------|
| sun | sunny |
| rain | rainy |
| wind | windy |
| cloud | cloudy |
| snow | snowy |
| fog | foggy |
| thunder | thundery |
| lightning | – |

It's a **sunny** day in Tokyo today, but it's **cloudy** in Hong Kong.
It's **foggy** in Vancouver, and it's **snowing** / it's **snowy** in Ottawa.
It's **raining** in São Paulo, but **the sun's shining** in Rio de Janeiro.

It's **beautiful** weather today. (*not* It's a beautiful weather.)
The weather is **awful** today.

You cannot say: It's ~~winding / clouding / fogging / sunning.~~

**C**  Other weather words

Here's the **weather forecast**. [a guess about what the weather is likely to be in the future]
It's very **hot** in Mexico – sometimes more than **100 degrees Fahrenheit (38 degrees Celsius)** in the summer.
It's very **cold** in the Arctic. It's often **minus 58 degrees Fahrenheit (minus 50 degrees Celsius)** there.
It's often **wet** in Seattle. Carry an umbrella when you go there.
It's very **dry** in the Sahara desert. It doesn't rain much there.

A **hurricane** is an extremely strong wind.
A **storm** has strong wind and rain together.
A **thunderstorm** is when there is thunder, lightning, rain, and sometimes wind.

> *tip*  *If you are able to check the **weather forecast** in English on the Internet, check it as often as you can.*

# Exercises

**37.1**   Match the words and the symbols.

1. snow    2. sun    3. rain    4. fog    5. lightning    6. wind    7. clouds

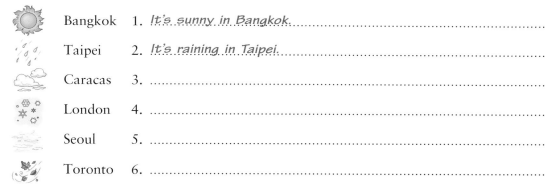

a.    b.    c.    d.

e.    f.    g.

**37.2**   Look at the types of weather in A on page 74. Write them down in order from your most favorite to your least favorite.

**37.3**   Write sentences about the places in the chart.

Bangkok    1. *It's sunny in Bangkok.*..........................................................................

Taipei    2. *It's raining in Taipei.*..........................................................................

Caracas    3. ..........................................................................................................

London    4. ..........................................................................................................

Seoul    5. ..........................................................................................................

Toronto    6. ..........................................................................................................

**37.4**   Complete these sentences with a word from page 74.

1. The sun was .....*shining*........ this morning.
2. When it ........................, I take my umbrella.
3. It's beautiful ........................ today.
4. It is ........................ now; maybe we can go skiing.
5. You see ........................ before you hear thunder.
6. It is dangerous to be in a small boat when there is a ........................ .
7. Go on the Internet to read the ........................ for tomorrow.

**37.5**   Are these sentences true about the weather in your country? If not, correct them.

1. It often snows in December.
2. It's usually 80 degrees Fahrenheit (27 degrees Celsius) in summer and 0 degrees Fahrenheit (−18 degrees Celsius) in winter.
3. There are thunderstorms every day in August.
4. It is very wet in spring.
5. We never have hurricanes.
6. Summer is my favorite season because it is usually hot and dry.

**37.6**   Write about the weather where you are today. Use as many words as possible from page 74.

### A Downtown

You can **get/take a train** at the **train station**.
You can **change money** at the **bank**.
You can **borrow books** and **read newspapers** at the **library**.
You can **check e-mail** at an **Internet café**.
You can **buy books** at a **bookstore**.
You can **park your car** in a **parking lot/garage**.

### B Streets and roads

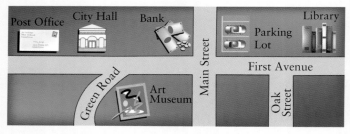

*Asking for help*
**Where's** City Hall? **How do I get** to Oak Street? **Is there** a pay phone nearby?
**Can I** park here? **Excuse me, I'm looking for** the museum.

### C People in the city

    police officer    taxi driver    salesclerk    librarian    bank teller

### D Signs

    no parking    no entry    bus stop    railroad crossing    signal ahead

# Exercises

**38.1** **Answer these questions about A on page 76.**

1. Where can I get a train to New York?   *At the train station.*
2. Where can I get information about hotels?
3. Where can I change money?
4. Where can I park?
5. Where can I see paintings?
6. Where can I check my e-mail?
7. Where can I buy a book?
8. Where can I read a book without buying it?

**38.2** **Look at the map in B on page 76. Ask questions that go with the answers on the right.**

1. *Where's the library?* ............ On First Avenue, near Oak Street.
2. ........................................? It's next to City Hall.
3. ........................................? Make a left on Green Road.
4. ........................................? The parking lot on First Avenue is best.
5. ........................................? There's a bank on Main Street.

**38.3** **Where do these people work?**

1. bus driver *..on a bus*
2. salesclerk .................................................
3. librarian .................................................
4. police officer .................................................
5. bank teller .................................................

**38.4** **What are these signs?**

1. .........................   3. .........................   5. .........................

2. .........................   4. .........................

**38.5** **Write a paragraph about what to see in your city or town. Use words from page 76.**

# In the country

The **country** (or **the countryside**) means *outside of cities or towns* and often includes farmland. **Country** can also mean a nation (e.g., Brazil, Japan, Italy).

## A Things you can see in the country

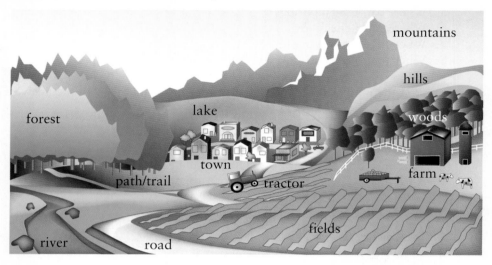

## B Living and working in the country

In the country, many people live in **towns**. [like a city but smaller]
A farmer lives **on a farm** and works **in the fields**.
My friend lives **in a cabin**. [a small, simple house in the country or mountains]

## C Nature

**Nature** means *everything in the natural world* (e.g., animals, birds, plants).
I love **nature**. (*not* I love ~~the~~ nature.)
I like walking **in the country**. (*not* I like walking in the ~~nature~~. *Nature* is not a place.)
Animals in their natural environment are called **wildlife**. (*Note: Wildlife* is an uncountable noun.)
There is lots of **wildlife** in the country.

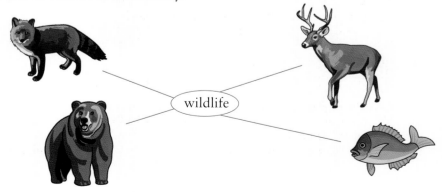

# Exercises

**39.1** Cover page 78. How many names of things in the country can you remember?

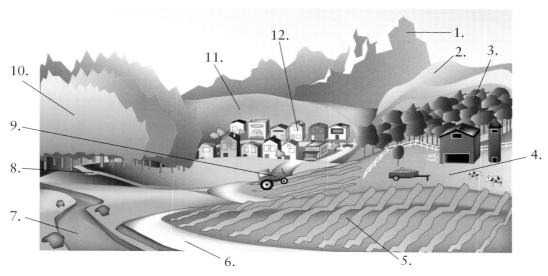

**39.2** Fill in the blanks.

1. My brother is a ......*farmer.*...... He lives ........................ a farm.
2. It's not a big house. It's just a ........................ .
3. The farm is near a small ........................ . A few hundred people live there.
4. We like to climb the ........................ near our house.
5. We went swimming in a ........................ near the farm. The water was warm.
6. There is some wonderful ........................ in this area, especially wild animals.
7. Let's go for a walk along the ........................ . It goes through the woods and down to the lake.

**39.3** Describe the typical countryside where you come from. Write at least four sentences about it. Use these questions to help you.

1. Are there any woods or forests?
2. Are there any hills or mountains?
3. Are there any lakes or rivers?
4. Are there many small towns?
5. Are there any farms?
6. Are there any trails where you can walk?
7. Can you see any wildlife?

**39.4** Write *the* in the sentence if necessary.

1. The farmer works all day in ........*the*........ fields.
2. He loves ........................ nature.
3. She wants to live in ........................ country.
4. They are interested in ........................ wildlife.
5. She likes to paint pictures of ........................ countryside.

# Pets and other animals

**A** Farm animals

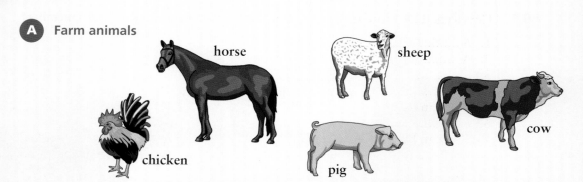

| Animal | Baby | Meat | Other products |
|---|---|---|---|
| cow | calf | beef, veal (from a calf) | leather, milk |
| sheep | lamb | mutton, lamb (from a lamb) | wool |
| pig | piglet | pork, bacon, ham | leather |
| chicken | chick | chicken | eggs |

**B** Wild or zoo animals

**C** Pets

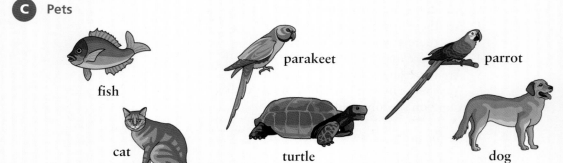

These animals are often **pets**. [animals that people keep in their homes]

Parrots and parakeets are **birds**.
You **take** your dog **for a walk**, but you don't usually take your cat for a walk.

# Exercises

**40.1** Complete these sentences with words from page 80.

1. A ....*turtle*.... moves very slowly.
2. A ................................. has a very long neck.
3. ............................. , ............................. , and ............................. are birds.
4. ............................. and ............................. are large cats.
5. You can ride a ............................. and an ............................. .
6. ............................. swim and ............................. fly.
7. You can buy ............................. at a butcher shop or a supermarket.
8. ............................. and ............................. give us food for breakfast.

**40.2** Match the animal on the left with its meat on the right.

*Animal*
1. chicken
2. calf
3. lamb
4. cow
5. pig

*Meat*
a. lamb
b. ham
c. beef
d. chicken
e. veal

**40.3** Look at the animals on page 80. Answer these questions.
1. Which animals eat meat?
2. Which animals give us things that we wear?
3. Which animals lay eggs?
4. Which animals in C are sometimes in a zoo?
5. Which animals in B are sometimes pets?

**40.4** Look at the pictures and complete the crossword puzzle.

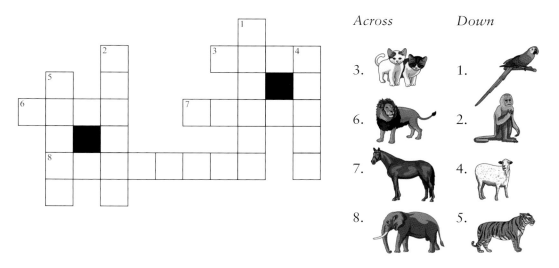

*Across*

3.
6.
7.
8.

*Down*

1.
2.
4.
5.

**40.5** There are 17 different animals in the pictures on page 80. Cover the page. How many of these animals can you remember?

# Travel

## A Types of transportation

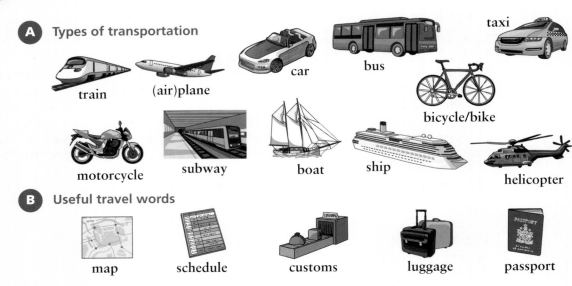

train    (air)plane    car    bus    taxi    bicycle/bike    motorcycle    subway    boat    ship    helicopter

## B Useful travel words

map    schedule    customs    luggage    passport

Can I have a **one-way / round-trip** ticket to Chicago, please?
   [one-way = Toronto → Chicago; round-trip = Toronto → Chicago → Toronto]
Do you have a **confirmation number**? [a number that shows you have a reservation]
How much is the train / bus / taxi / air **fare**?
Is it a long **trip**? (*not* Is it a long ~~travel~~?)

## C Plane

You can print your **boarding pass** [paper you need to get on a plane] at home from the Internet or receive it at the airport.

To **check in**, [tell the airline that you are in the airport] you must arrive at least two hours before the plane **takes off**. [leaves the ground]

Do you have any **carry-on luggage**? [bags small enough for you to take on the plane]

You can **check your luggage/bags** before the flight. [leave your luggage to be taken onto the plane] After you arrive, you pick up your luggage at the **baggage claim** area.

The plane arrives at **Gate** 9. Have a good **flight**. [trip on an airplane]

The plane **landed** [arrived] in Chicago at 5:30.

## D Car

We **rented a car** for a week.
We had to **fill** it **up with gas**.

I'm going into town. Do you want **a ride**? [go with someone in their car]

## E Train

The train arriving at **Platform** 3 is the 4:50 to Washington, D.C.

The Philadelphia train **departs/leaves from** Platform 6.

Is there a **dining car** [a special car where passengers can eat] on this train?

Do I have to **change trains**? [get off one train and get onto another]

# Exercises

**41.1** **Match the words on the left with their definitions on the right.**

| | |
|---|---|
| 1. land | a. to let the airline know you are in the airport |
| 2. fare | b. the paper you need to get on a plane |
| 3. dining car | c. it says when planes/trains depart and arrive |
| 4. ship | d. what you pay for travel |
| 5. schedule | e. when a plane arrives at an airport |
| 6. gate | f. it travels on water, e.g., the *Titanic* |
| 7. boarding pass | g. the number that shows you have a reservation |
| 8. confirmation number | h. where you stand when you are waiting for a train |
| 9. check in | i. a place to eat on a train |
| 10. platform | j. where a plane arrives |

**41.2** **Answer these questions about travel.**

1. What is the difference between a one-way ticket and a round-trip ticket?
2. What do you get at the baggage claim area of an airport?
3. Does a plane take off at the end of a trip? (If not, what does it do?)
4. What is the difference between renting a car and buying a car?
5. What do you do when you check your luggage?
6. If you only have carry-on luggage do you check any bags?

**41.3** **Complete the crossword puzzle.**

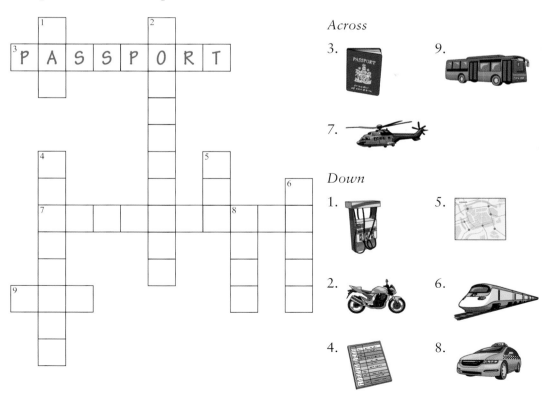

*Across*

3. 9.

7.

*Down*

1. 5.

2. 6.

4. 8.

## A Going in and going out

You go in here.   You go out here.

## B Warnings and caution

No smoking here    No parking here

## C Other useful signs

There are lots of different signs for public **restrooms** (bathrooms).

 Men
Gentlemen

 Women
Ladies

*tip* *Look for other signs in English. Write down any that you see.*

# Exercises

**42.1** Match the signs on the left with their opposites on the right.

1.

a.

2.

b.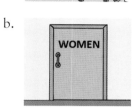

3.

c.

4.

d.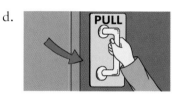

**42.2** Choose the correct letter.

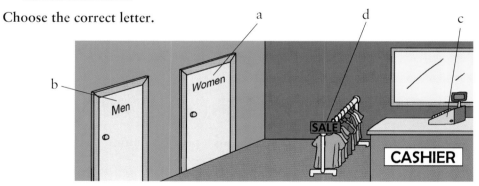

1. You want to buy something for less than full price.
2. You want to pay for something.
3. Your father wants to go to the restroom.
4. Your sister wants to go to the restroom.

**42.3** Look at each of the signs and notices on page 84. Write down a place where you can see each of them.

*Out of order – on a pay phone*

# Food and drink

### A Everyday food

Would you like some **bread**?
   (*not* Would you like a bread?)
In Asia, many people eat **rice**.
Spaghetti is a type of **pasta**.
Some people eat **meat** or **fish** every day.
What do you want **for dessert** – **ice cream** or **cake**?

### B Fast food

**Fast food** is often hot food, prepared and served quickly in informal restaurants called fast-food restaurants. Some popular fast foods are:

hamburger      (French) fries      hot dog      pizza

Sometimes fast food is called **junk food** because it's not always good for you.
(**Junk** can mean anything that is useless or of low quality.)

### C Fruit and vegetables

carrots   banana   potatoes   pineapple   peas   grapes   garlic   apple

oranges   mushrooms   green beans   pear   onions   strawberries   tomatoes

### D Drinks

coffee         tea         milk      juice      soda/pop      mineral water /
                                                              sparking water

*tip*   Go to a grocery store / supermarket. How many types of food and drink
        have English names on them? Try to learn some of them.

# Exercises

**43.1**  Complete these sentences with words from A and B on page 86.

1. ......*Rice*...... is an important food in Japan.
2. Potatoes are used to make ........................................ .
3. Macaroni, spaghetti, and linguine are all types of ........................................ .
4. Beef is used to make ........................................ , a popular fast food.
5. Ice cream and cake are popular types of ........................................ .
6. ........................................ and ........................................ are sometimes called fast food.
7. ........................................ is a popular fast food, usually made with lots of cheese.
8. Some people bake their own ........................................ .

**43.2**  Write these words in the correct column. Then add two more items to each list.

| pineapple | green bean | carrot | grape | onion | apple |
|-----------|------------|--------|-------|-------|-------|
| orange | banana | garlic | pear | mushroom | |

| *Fruit* | *Vegetables* |
|---------|--------------|
| pineapple | |
| | |

**43.3**  There are six drinks in the puzzle. Can you find them?

```
A  J  A  N  O  W  S
J  U (S  O  D  A) I
M  I  L  K  A  T  T
U  C  O  F  F  E  E
T  E  M  L  O  R  A
```

**43.4**  What are your three favorite things to eat and your three favorite things to drink?
Which ones are good for you? Use a dictionary if you need help.

# In the kitchen

**A**  What's in the kitchen?

sink  microwave  faucet  cabinet / cupboard  stove  freezer  oven  refrigerator  counter  dishwasher

**B**  Things you use in the kitchen

dish soap / dish detergent    pot    paper towels

dishtowel    frying pan    teapot    coffeemaker

**C**  Things you use for eating and drinking

cup    plate/dish    knife    chopsticks    glass

saucer    bowl    fork    spoon    mug

**D**  Questions in the kitchen

Where can I find a mug / a dishtowel / some paper towels?
Can I help with the dishes / the cooking?
Where does this cup / dish / frying pan go? [Where do you keep it?]
Where should I put this cup / the sugar?

# Exercises

**44.1**

| Check (✓) yes or no. | Yes | No |
|---|---|---|
| 1. I use a frying pan to drink out of. | | ✓ |
| 2. Dish soap makes the dishes clean. | | |
| 3. The refrigerator is cold inside. | | |
| 4. The freezer is not as cold as the refrigerator. | | |
| 5. I turn on the faucet to get water. | | |
| 6. A dishtowel is for making plates wet. | | |
| 7. You can use paper towels to clean the counter. | | |

**44.2** **What do you need to do these tasks?**

1. Make coffee *I need coffee, water, a coffeemaker, a cup, a spoon.* ........................
2. Make tea ................................................................................................
3. Fry an egg ...............................................................................................
4. Eat food .................................................................................................
5. Drink some water .....................................................................................
6. Cook dinner in just two minutes ................................................................

**44.3** **Look at the picture and complete the dialogs.**

1.  A: *Can I help with the dishes?*
    B: Thanks. I'll wash the plates and
    you can put them away.
2.  A: Is there any milk?
    B: ......................................................
3.  A: Where does the coffeemaker go?
    B: ......................................................

4.  A: ............................................................. ?
    B: It's in the freezer.
5.  A: Do you have a dishwasher?
    B: ......................................................
6.  A: Where is the cake?
    B: ......................................................

# In the bedroom and bathroom

**A** **Bedroom**

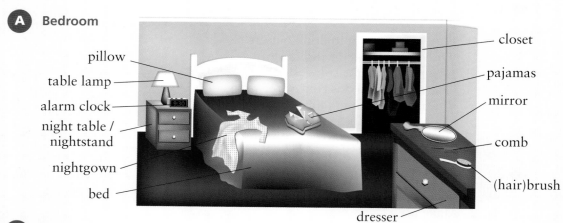

- pillow
- table lamp
- alarm clock
- night table / nightstand
- nightgown
- bed
- closet
- pajamas
- mirror
- comb
- (hair)brush
- dresser

**B** **Bathroom**

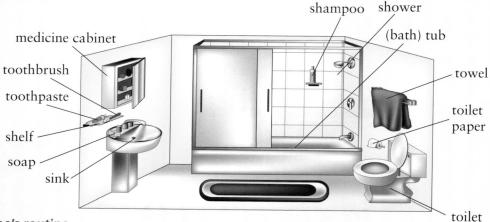

- medicine cabinet
- toothbrush
- toothpaste
- shelf
- soap
- sink
- shampoo
- shower
- (bath) tub
- towel
- toilet paper
- toilet

**C** **Joe's routine**

Joe usually **goes to bed** at 11 o'clock.
He **washes his face** and **gets undressed**.
He **gets into bed** and reads for a little while. Then he **turns off** the light and **falls asleep**.
He **wakes up** when his alarm clock rings.
He **gets up** and goes to the bathroom.
He **takes a shower** and **brushes his teeth**.
He **gets dressed** and **eats breakfast**.
(See Unit 12 for verbs for everyday actions.)

# Exercises

**45.1**  Look at the picture and write the nouns next to the numbers.

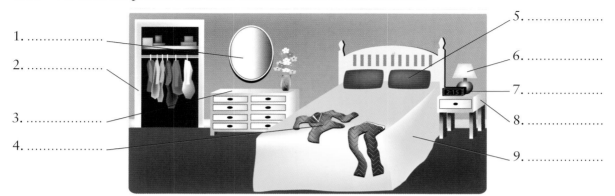

1. ....................
2. ....................
3. ....................
4. ....................

5. ....................
6. ....................
7. ....................
8. ....................
9. ....................

**45.2**  Write down five more things that you need to take with you if you go to stay with a friend for one night.

*toothbrush* ....................     ....................     ....................

....................     ....................     ....................

**45.3**  Look at the pictures. Describe what the people are doing.

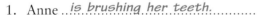

1. Anne *is brushing her teeth.* ....................

4. Luis .................... .

2. Aya .................... .

5. James .................... .

3. Mr. and Mrs. Park .................... .

6. Antonio .................... .

**45.4**  Write about your nighttime and morning routines. Look at the verbs in C on page 90 if you need help. Think about these questions to help you.

When do you usually go to bed?    *I usually go to bed at 10.*
When do you usually wake up?
Do you shower in the morning or at night?

**A** Things in the living room

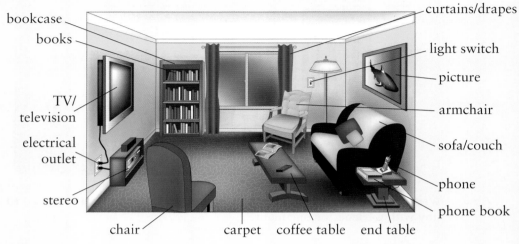

bookcase
books
TV/television
electrical outlet
stereo
chair
carpet
coffee table
end table
curtains/drapes
light switch
picture
armchair
sofa/couch
phone
phone book

**B** Things you use

Where is **the remote / remote control** for the TV?
There's **a reading lamp** on the desk.
**Close the curtains** and **turn on the light**. It's getting dark.
Please **turn on the TV**. I want to watch the news.

**C** Things you do in the living room

Every night **I watch TV**.
Sometimes **I listen to music**.
Sometimes **I read**.
Sometimes I just **relax**.
    [rest and do nothing]

**D** Useful prepositions

The armchair is **near** the window.
The sofa is **next to** an end table.
The bookcase is **in the corner**.

The coffee table is **in the middle of** the room.
The bookcase is **against** the wall.
The stereo is **under** the TV.

# Exercises

**46.1**   **Answer these questions.**

1. Where can you put books? ..*a bookcase*.................................................................
2. Where can two or three people sit? .......................................................................
3. Where can you put down your coffee cup? ............................................................
4. What can you look at on the wall? .........................................................................
5. What turns the light on or off? ..............................................................................
6. What do you use to listen to music? ......................................................................
7. What often covers the floor in a room? .................................................................

**46.2**   **Choose (a), (b), or (c).**

1. If you want to lie back and relax, which is best?
   (a) a chair                     (b) an armchair                  (c) a sofa
2. If it is dark and you want to read, what do you do?
   (a) close the curtains          (b) switch on the reading lamp  (c) turn off the light
3. If you want to watch a different TV station, what do you do?
   (a) use the remote control      (b) use the electrical outlet    (c) turn off the TV
4. If you want to find a phone number, what do you need?
   (a) a remote control            (b) a phone book                 (c) a stereo

**46.3**   **Fill in the blanks with the correct prepositions. Look at the picture of the living room in A on page 92.**

1. There is a carpet ..........*on*.......... the floor.
2. There is a small table ......................... the corner. There is a phone .........................
   the table.
3. The TV is ......................... the chair.
4. The bookcase is ......................... the wall.
5. The stereo is ......................... the TV.

**46.4**   **Draw a picture of your living room at home. Then, write a paragraph about it. Think about these questions to help you.**

What color is your couch/sofa? Where is it?

Do you have any pictures on the walls?

What do you do when you are in your living room?

**A** What's his/her job?

doctor    teacher    nurse    lawyer    mechanic

salesclerk    hairdresser    farmer    receptionist

**B** Talking about jobs

What **do** you **do**? (What's your **job**?)
    I'm a waiter. / I'm a waitress.
Where do you **work**?
    I work in a restaurant.
Is it an interesting **job**?
    Yes, I like it.

waiter    waitress

**C** Workplaces

I work **in** a **factory** / an **office** / a **store** / a **hospital** / a **hair salon** / a **classroom** / a **court**.
I work **at/from** home.
I work **on** a **farm**.

# Exercises

**47.1** **Match the pictures with the jobs in the box.**

| farmer | lawyer | hairdresser | mechanic | nurse | receptionist |

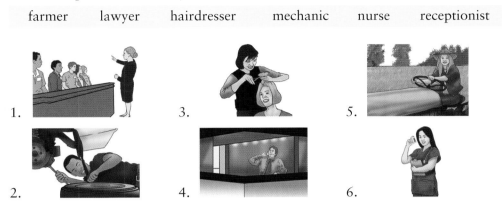

1.          3.          5.

2.          4.          6.

**47.2** **Fill in the letters in the crossword puzzle.**

*Across*
5. Works on a bus
6. Works in a school

*Down*
1. Works in a store
2. Works in a hospital
3. Works in a restaurant
4. Works with a doctor

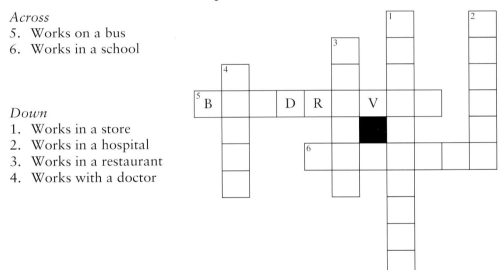

**47.3** **Fill in the blanks with words from page 94.**

Hank is a (1) .......*farmer.*...... He spends most of his day driving a tractor. When his tractor is not working, he takes it to a (2) ......................... . Hank's sister works in a store as a (3) ......................... . At night she is taking classes so that she can become a (4) ......................... and work in a hospital. Hank's other sister likes to cut hair. She is a (5) ......................... and owns her own shop.

**47.4** **Answer these questions about yourself. If you don't have a job, give answers about a friend or family member.**

1. What do you do?
2. Where do you work?
3. Is it an interesting job?

# School

## A Subjects

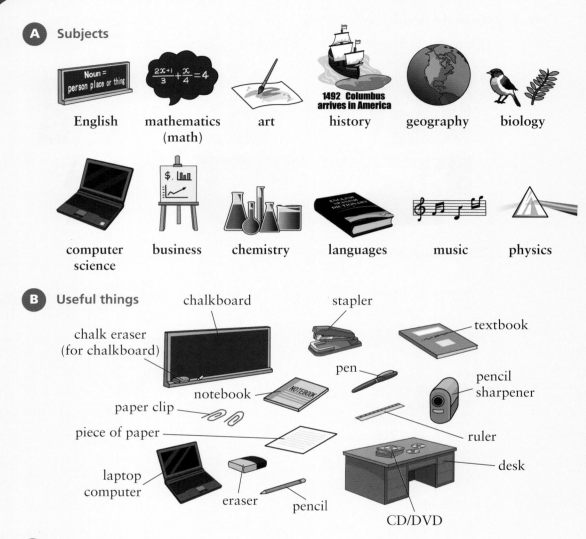

**English**

**mathematics (math)**

**art**

**history**

**geography**

**biology**

**computer science**

**business**

**chemistry**

**languages**

**music**

**physics**

## B Useful things

chalkboard

stapler

chalk eraser (for chalkboard)

textbook

pen

pencil sharpener

notebook

paper clip

piece of paper

ruler

laptop computer

desk

eraser

pencil

CD/DVD

## C Useful verbs

A math teacher **teaches** math. His/Her students **study** math.
After school, students **do** their **homework**.
In elementary school, children **learn** to read and write.
In college/university, a teacher/professor **gives a lecture**, and the students **take notes**.
Students **take courses/classes** in colleges and schools.
At the end of a course, you often have to **take an exam**.
You hope to **pass** your **tests and exams**.
You don't want to **fail** your **exams/tests**.
If you complete your courses at a college, you **graduate** and **get a degree**.

Bachelor of Arts
awarded to
David Lee
by West College

# Exercises

**48.1** Match the subjects on the left with the examples on the right.

| | | |
|---|---|---|
| 1. math | a. | animals and plants |
| 2. physics | b. | money |
| 3. history | c. | $12x + 18y = 7z$ |
| 4. geography | d. | $E = mc^2$ |
| 5. business | e. | $H_2O$ |
| 6. English | f. | the countries of the world |
| 7. chemistry | g. | the fifteenth century |
| 8. biology | h. | Spanish, Japanese, German |
| 9. computer science | i. | vocabulary |
| 10. languages | j. | the Internet |

**48.2** Look at the picture for 30 seconds. Then cover it. How many of the eight objects can you remember? Write them down in English.

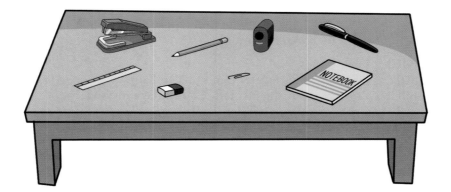

**48.3** Fill in the blanks with verbs from C on page 96. Put the verbs in the correct form.

Carla does well in school. It's easy for her to (1) ........ *learn* ........ , and she always (2) ........................ her homework. She (3) ........................ all her tests. She is in college, and (4) ........................ biology. She is also (5) ........................ a special chemistry course. Carla likes to sit in classes, listen to the lecturer, and (6) ........................ notes. She will (7) ........................ her final exams next month. If she (8) ............................. , she will (9) ........................ a degree in biology. If she (10) ........................ , she will be very sad. She would like to become a biology teacher.

**48.4** Look at the subjects in A on page 96. Which are your favorite subjects? Which ones are not your favorites? Give some reasons for each answer.

*My favorite subjects are...*

# Communications

## A  *Call, text, and fax*

cell phone    text (message)    (tele)phone    pay phone    fax (machine)    fax

Juan **makes** a lot of **phone calls**. He **calls** his girlfriend every day.

Ahmed just **sent** me a **text (message)**.
I'll **text** him later.

Amporn **sent** me a **fax** yesterday. / Amporn **faxed** me yesterday.
A: What's your **phone number** / **fax number**?
B: It's 555-0718 (*Note*: say *five-five-five, oh-seven-one-eight*).

## B  A typical phone conversation

NICK:  Hello?
SUE:  Hi, Nick. This is Sue. Can I talk to Kim?
NICK:  I'm sorry, but she just left. **Can I take a message?**
SUE:  Yeah, could you tell her I called? I'll call back later.
NICK:  OK. I'll tell her.
SUE:  Thanks. Bye.
NICK:  Bye.

## C  *E-mail*

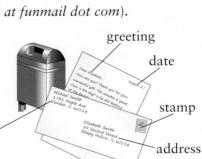

Anna gets a lot of **e-mail**.

A: Did you **e-mail** Pascual?
B: Yes, I **sent** him an **e-mail** yesterday.

A: What is your **e-mail address**?
B: It's sandy82@funmail.com (*Note*: say *Sandy 82 at funmail dot com*).

## D  Letters

Don't forget to put a **stamp** on the **envelope**.
Don't forget to **mail** the letters.

 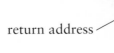

greeting
date
stamp
return address
address

# Exercises

**49.1** Answer these questions.

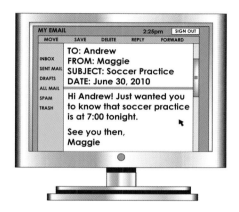

1. Who sent the e-mail?
2. What is in the e-mail's subject line?
3. Who is the e-mail to?

4. What is the fax number for Fit Gym?
5. Who sent the fax?
6. When did Fit Gym get the fax?

**49.2** Complete this conversation between Josh and Sara.

JOSH: Hi Sara. Did Amy send you a (1) m ........................... about the party tomorrow?

SARA: Yes, but I can't go. My brother is coming over to help me put in a (2) f ........................... machine.

JOSH: Do you want me to (3) t ........................... Amy and let her know you can't go?

SARA: No, I sent her an (4) e ........................... .

**49.3** Complete this chart to show how you communicate with these people and places. Use O for *often*, S for *sometimes*, N for *never*.

|  | *Write an e-mail* | *Send a fax* | *Write a letter* | *Make a phone call* | *Send a text message* |
|---|---|---|---|---|---|
| parents |  |  |  |  |  |
| professors |  |  |  |  |  |
| restaurant |  |  |  |  |  |
| government office |  |  |  |  |  |
| friends |  |  |  |  |  |

# Taking a trip

**A** **Vacation**

You can . . .
> **take** a vacation.
> **have** a vacation.
> **go on** vacation.
> **be on** vacation.

**B** **Transportation**

We're **going to drive / take the train/bus.** (See Units 14 and 41.)
Are you **flying** to Seattle from Vancouver?
No, we're **taking the ferry.** [a ship where you can take your car with you]

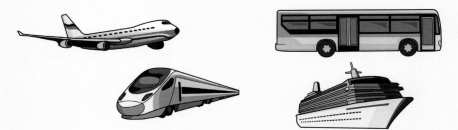

**C** **Things to remember to take**

your **passport** (if you are going to another country)
a **visa** [a special stamp in your passport to go to some countries]
your **tickets**
**credit cards** and some **local currency** [money of the country you're going to]
a **camera**
a **guidebook** [a book that gives visitors information about a country]
your **luggage** [suitcases, bags, etc.]

**D** **When you are there**

send some **postcards**
try the **local food**
enjoy the **nightlife** [discos, clubs, etc.]
go to the **tourist information office/center**
> if you have any questions
**have a good time** [enjoy your vacation]

# Exercises

**50.1** **Choose (a), (b), or (c).**

1. Next week I will be .............. vacation.
   (a) in          (b) on          (c) off
2. Cristina works too much, she should .............. a vacation.
   (a) go          (b) be          (c) take
3. Jake .............. a great vacation in Thailand.
   (a) went        (b) had         (c) made
4. My neighbors go .............. vacation every summer.
   (a) on          (b) in          (c) to

**50.2** **Write the names of these things you may need on a trip.**

1. ......*guidebook*........       3. ..................................       5. ..................................

2. ..................................       4. ..................................       6. ..................................

**50.3** **Match the descriptions on the left with the words on the right.**

1. A card that lets you buy something now and pay for it later
2. A special stamp or paper in your passport so that you can enter a country.
3. Cards with pictures that you mail to friends and family
4. Discos, clubs, and other entertainment at night
5. A place where you can get information about places to see
6. The dishes typical of a region

a. tourist information office

b. local food

c. credit card

d. visa

e. postcards

f. nightlife

**50.4** **You are going on vacation. Think about how you will get there. Answer these questions.**

1. Which is usually faster – a car or a ferry?
2. Which is usually cheaper – taking the bus or taking the train?
3. Which can you take more luggage on – a ferry or a plane?
4. Which one often lets you see more as you travel – a car or a bus?

# Shopping

## A  Kinds of stores

hardware store

grocery store / supermarket

bookstore

bakery

gift shop

toy store

post office

drugstore

electronics store

## B  Department store

A **department store** is a large store that sells different things (e.g., **clothes**, **furniture**, **stationery** [pens, paper, etc.], **cosmetics** [beauty products, makeup]).

| Directory | JD NICHOLS | Directory |
|---|---|---|
| **BASEMENT** Food Sports Equipment | **SECOND FLOOR** Women's Clothing | **FOURTH FLOOR** Electronics Furniture |
| **MAIN FLOOR** Cosmetics, Shoes Stationery | **THIRD FLOOR** Children's Clothes Toys, Menswear | **FIFTH FLOOR** Garden Restaurant |

## C  Going shopping

A **salesclerk/salesperson** helps you find things and sells you things.
You pay for things at the **cashier / cash register**.
You get a **receipt**. [a piece of paper the cashier gives you that shows what you bought and the price]

## D  Useful phrases

A:  Can I help you?
B:  Yes. How much does this **cost**?

Can I pay **by check**   *or*   **use a credit card**?
No, **cash** only.

cash

coins/change

A:  I need some coins for the parking meter. Do you have any **change**?
B:  Sorry, I only have dollar **bills**. [paper money, not coins]

Can I **try it on**? [put on clothes to see how they look or fit]
Do you have **a larger size / a smaller size / a different color**?

check book

credit card

Would you like a **bag**?

# Exercises

**51.1** Match the item with the store.

| toy store | hardware store | bakery | gift shop | drugstore | electronics store |

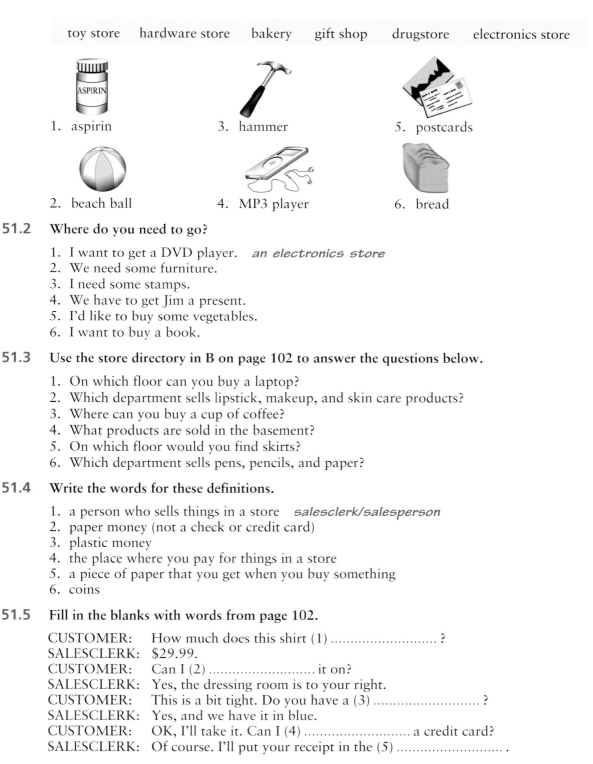

1. aspirin

2. beach ball

3. hammer

4. MP3 player

5. postcards

6. bread

**51.2** Where do you need to go?

1. I want to get a DVD player.    *an electronics store*
2. We need some furniture.
3. I need some stamps.
4. We have to get Jim a present.
5. I'd like to buy some vegetables.
6. I want to buy a book.

**51.3** Use the store directory in B on page 102 to answer the questions below.

1. On which floor can you buy a laptop?
2. Which department sells lipstick, makeup, and skin care products?
3. Where can you buy a cup of coffee?
4. What products are sold in the basement?
5. On which floor would you find skirts?
6. Which department sells pens, pencils, and paper?

**51.4** Write the words for these definitions.

1. a person who sells things in a store    *salesclerk/salesperson*
2. paper money (not a check or credit card)
3. plastic money
4. the place where you pay for things in a store
5. a piece of paper that you get when you buy something
6. coins

**51.5** Fill in the blanks with words from page 102.

CUSTOMER:     How much does this shirt (1) .......................... ?
SALESCLERK:  $29.99.
CUSTOMER:     Can I (2) .......................... it on?
SALESCLERK:  Yes, the dressing room is to your right.
CUSTOMER:     This is a bit tight. Do you have a (3) .......................... ?
SALESCLERK:  Yes, and we have it in blue.
CUSTOMER:     OK, I'll take it. Can I (4) .......................... a credit card?
SALESCLERK:  Of course. I'll put your receipt in the (5) .......................... .

## A  At the reception desk (the front desk)

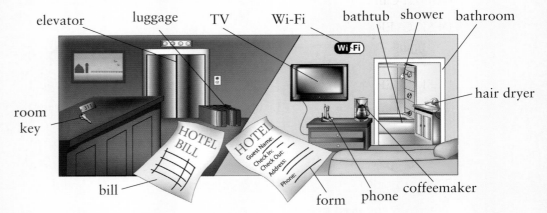

When you arrive at a hotel you can say:
> I'd like to **check in**.
> I have a **reservation**. [I booked/reserved a room in advance.]
> My **confirmation number** is 5149. [a number to locate your reservation]

If you don't have a reservation you can say:
> I'd like a **single room** [for one person] / a **double room**. [for two people]
> How much is a single room?
> I'd like a **nonsmoking room**, if possible. [Smoking is not allowed.]

The desk clerk may say:
> Your room is on the **ninth floor**. The **elevator** is over there.
> Here is your **room key**.
> Would you like some help with your **luggage**?
> Could you **fill out** this **form**, please?
> **Sign** here, please. [Write your name to show you agree to the hotel rules.]

When you leave, you say:
> I'm **checking out** now.
> Can I have the **bill**, please?

## B  Hotel services

Can I have **room service**, please? [Someone brings food/drink to your room.]
Can I have a **wake-up call** at 6:30 a.m., please? [You want a telephone call to wake you up at 6:30 a.m.]
Is there **valet parking**? [Someone parks your car for you.]
Is there an **Internet connection**?
Is there a **concierge**? [someone who performs special services like arranging tours and making dinner reservations for guests]
Is there a **dry-cleaning** service? [special way of cleaning clothes, especially fancy clothes]

# Exercises

**52.1** Look at the pictures and complete the conversation with words from page 104.

GUEST: Can I have a [image] (1) ........*double*...... room for tonight, please?

DESK CLERK: Would you like a [image] (2) ........................ room?

GUEST: Yes, please. And does the room have an [image] (3) ........................ ?

DESK CLERK: All our rooms have wireless Internet, a [image] (4) ........................ ,

and a [image] (5) ........................ . I can give you Room 225. It's on the second

[image] (6) ........................ . Here is your [image] (7) ........................ .

The [image] (8) ........................ is over there. Do you need help with your

[image] 9) ........................ ?

GUEST: No, thank you. Can I have a copy of my [image] (10) ........................ ?

DESK CLERK: Yes, I'll give it to you tomorrow when you check out.

**52.2** Match what you want with what you need.

*You want:*
1. to have coffee in your room
2. to go to the top floor
3. to unlock your door
4. to get up at 6 a.m.
5. to check your e-mail
6. to watch the news
7. to wash your hair
8. to dry your hair
9. to eat a meal in your room
10. to confirm your reservation

*You need:*
a. the elevator
b. an Internet connection
c. a shower
d. a coffeemaker
e. a hair dryer
f. a wake-up call
g. a confirmation number
h. room service
i. a room key
j. a TV

**52.3** Put a check mark (✓) under the hotels that have the following services.

| Service | A cheap hotel | An average hotel | A luxury hotel |
|---|---|---|---|
| room service | | ✓ | ✓ |
| wake-up call | | | |
| valet parking | | | |
| Internet connection | | | |
| concierge | | | |
| dry cleaning | | | |

**52.4** Write six questions that you can ask in a hotel beginning with *Can I . . .*

*Can I have a wake-up call, please?*

# Eating out

## A Places where you can eat

**café:** You can have coffee or tea and a **snack** there. [something small to eat like a sandwich or a piece of cake] They sometimes serve meals there, too. Some cafés let you sit at your table for a long period of time.

**coffee shop:** A small restaurant that serves inexpensive meals, coffee/tea, etc.

**deli:** A store that sells cooked meats, cheese, salads, and sandwiches that you can take out to eat in a different place.

**fast-food restaurant:** You can get a quick hot meal there (e.g., a hamburger and French fries). (See Unit 43 on food and drink.)

**restaurant:** You go there for a complete meal; often more expensive than a café.

## B In a restaurant – the menu

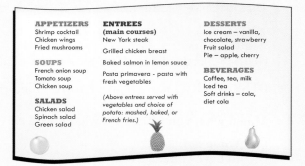

**APPETIZERS**
Shrimp cocktail
Chicken wings
Fried mushrooms

**SOUPS**
French onion soup
Tomato soup
Chicken soup

**SALADS**
Chicken salad
Spinach salad
Green salad

**ENTREES**
**(main courses)**
New York steak

Grilled chicken breast

Baked salmon in lemon sauce

Pasta primavera - pasta with fresh vegetables

*(Above entrees served with vegetables and choice of potato: mashed, baked, or French fries.)*

**DESSERTS**
Ice cream – vanilla, chocolate, strawberry
Fruit salad
Pie – apple, cherry

**BEVERAGES**
Coffee, tea, milk
Iced tea
Soft drinks – cola, diet cola

The **entree** is the main dish of the meal.

A **soft drink** (also called **soda** or **pop**) is a sweet-flavored drink without alcohol, e.g., cola.

**Vegetarian options:** These menu items do not have meat (e.g., beef, chicken or pork).

## C Ordering food

WAITRESS:   Are you ready to order?
CUSTOMER: Yes. I'll have the shrimp cocktail to start, and steak for the main course.
WAITRESS:   Would you like mashed potatoes, baked potato, or French fries?
CUSTOMER: I'll have the French fries, please.
WAITRESS:   How would you like your steak – rare, medium, or well-done?
CUSTOMER: Well-done.
WAITRESS:   And what would you like to drink?
CUSTOMER: Iced tea, please.
*(later)*
WAITRESS:   Is everything all right?
CUSTOMER: Yes, everything's fine, thanks. Can we have the check?
WAITERESS: Sure, here it is.
CUSTOMER: Is service included?
WAITRESS:   No, it isn't.
CUSTOMER: OK, I'll add the tip then.

> *tip* **Sometimes restaurants in other countries have English menus for tourists. Look at one of these. Write down any useful words you find.**

# Exercises

**53.1**  Match the descriptions on the left with the places to eat on the right.

1. You want to get a sandwich to eat in your office.
2. You want a romantic dinner for two.
3. You want a hamburger or a quick meal.
4. You want to sit and drink coffee while you read the paper.
5. You want a quick cup of coffee.

a. café
b. fast-food restaurant
c. deli
d. coffee shop
e. restaurant

**53.2**  Do you have all the places from A on page 106 in your country? Write down all the eating places you have. Give an example of a place of this type.

*fast-food restaurant – McDonald's*

**53.3**  Answer these questions. Look at the menu on page 106.

1. What would you order from the menu as an entree?
2. What would a vegetarian eat?
3. Can you find four things on the menu made with chicken?
4. Which one is a soft drink: coffee, milk, or cola?

**53.4**  Complete the sentences with one of the words in the box.

| steak | beverage | potato | ice cream | soup | salad |
|---|---|---|---|---|---|

1. You can have tomato, vegetable, or chicken ........*soup*........ to start.
2. Which ...................... do you want soda, coffee, or tea?
3. I'll have the fruit ...................... .
4. Do you want a baked ...................... or French fries?
5. Do you like your ...................... well-done, medium, or rare?
6. Can I have the chocolate ...................... , please?

**53.5**  Correct the mistakes in this conversation.

WAITER:  Are you ready ~~for~~ *to* order?
CUSTOMER: Yes. I like the French onion soup and a hamburger, please.
WAITER:  What would you like your hamburger – rare, medium, or done good?
CUSTOMER: Medium.
WAITER:  Anything to drink?
CUSTOMER: I have an iced tea, please.

**53.6**  Cover page 106 and write down all the words you can remember. Then look at the page again and write down any words you forgot.

**A** Ball games

People **play** all these sports. I **play** golf. Do you **play** tennis?

 soccer

 football

 tennis

 basketball

baseball     volleyball     golf     table tennis (Ping-Pong)

**B** Other popular sports

I **run** every day. She **bowls** every Sunday. You can also use **go** with most of these sports. I **go running** every day. She **goes bowling** every Sunday.

swimming     running     sailing     ice skating

bowling     cycling     judo/karate     skiing

*Note*: Use **do** with judo and karate: He **does** judo. I **do** karate. (See Unit 4 for the use of **go**.)

**C** Asking questions about sports

**Do you play any sports?** Yes, I swim / cycle / sail / bowl.
**Do you play** soccer / football / tennis / volleyball?
**What's your favorite sport?** I like ice skating **best**.

**D** Where we play sports

You play tennis/volleyball/basketball on a **court**. You golf on a **course**.
You play football/soccer/baseball on a **field**. You swim / go swimming in a s**wimming pool**.
You bowl / go bowling at the **bowling alley**. You ice-skate / go ice skating at a **rink**.

> *tip*    *Make a page in your vocabulary book for "sports." Read about sports on an English-language Web site. Write down the names of sports you do not know. Look them up in a dictionary.*

# Exercises

**54.1** Cover page 108 and try to remember the names of these sports.

1. *cycling* 3. .................................. 5. ..................................

  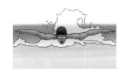

2. .................................. 4. .................................. 6. ..................................

**54.2** Which sports do you think of when you see these pictures?

1. .................................. 3. .................................. 5. ..................................

2. .................................. 4. .................................. 6. ..................................

**54.3** Ask questions for these answers.

1. *Why do you do karate / like karate* .................................................?
   Because it's great exercise and it's good for self-defense.

2. .................................................................................?
   I like running best.

3. .................................................................................?
   No, I don't play any at all. I prefer watching TV.

4. .................................................................................?
   Yes. I swim every Friday.

**54.4** Match the sport on the left with the place it is played on the right.

1. volleyball       a. a pool
2. football         b. a course
3. ice skating      c. a court
4. golf             d. a field
5. swimming         e. a rink

**54.5** Write the names of sports you have played. Which ones do you like?
Which do you not like? Which ones would you like to try?

# Movies

## A Types of movies

a Western    a comedy    a science fiction movie    an action movie    a musical    a thriller

a romantic comedy    a cartoon / an animated film    a horror movie    a detective movie    a love story / romantic movie

A: Do you like **Westerns**?
B: Not really; I like **comedies** best.
The best **science fiction movie** I've ever seen was *Journey to the Center of the Earth*.
If I see a **horror movie**, I can't sleep.

## B People in movies

Tom Cruise is a **movie star**. He lives in Hollywood.
He is **in** the *Mission Impossible* movies.
Sean Connery **played** James Bond in *Goldfinger*
   and other early 007 movies.

I like movies by Japanese **directors**.

## C Watching movies

Do you **go to the movies** often?
   Yes, I go all the time.
   No, I mostly **watch movies** at home.
**What's in** the movie theaters this week? What's **playing** this week?
   There's a new Disney animated film.
**Have** you **seen** the latest Batman movie?
   Yes, I saw it **on TV**.
Did you like *Titanic*?
   Yes, **I loved it / enjoyed it**.
   No, it was **boring**. [makes you want to fall asleep]

*tip*   *You can learn a lot of vocabulary by reading the names of movies. Find the names of new movies online. Write any new words in your vocabulary notebook.*

# Exercises

**55.1** **What types of movies are these?**

1. Some cowboys rob a train. *Western*
2. A man wakes up in the year 2150.
3. A dead person comes back to life.
4. James Bond saves the world.
5. Mickey Mouse goes to the movies.
6. A man falls in love with his neighbor.
7. A bank is robbed, and the bank robbers get away . . . or do they?
8. There is a lot of singing and dancing.

**55.2** **How many words for other types of movies can you make with the letters of ROMANTIC? Fill in the blanks.**

<pre>
T __ **R** __ __ L __ __
     __ **O** __ __ __ R
C __ **M** __ __ Y
       **A** __ T __ __ N
S __ __ **N** C __ F __ __ __ __ __ N
W __ __ **T** __ __ N
M __ __ **I** C __ L
       **C** A __ __ O O __
</pre>

**55.3** **Fill in the blanks.**

1. Do you prefer to go ......................... movies or to watch TV?
2. We ......................... a movie last night.
3. Who ......................... James Bond in *You Only Live Twice*?
4. Was Marlon Brando ......................... *The Godfather*?
5. A lot of big ......................... live in Hollywood.
6. Steven Spielberg is a famous movie ......................... .

**55.4** **Answer these questions about yourself.**

1. Name one science fiction movie you have seen.
2. Who is your favorite movie star?
3. Do you like detective movies? Can you name one?
4. Can you watch horror movies?
5. What's playing in the movie theater in your town?

**55.5** **Try to name one example of each type of movie from A on page 110!**

# Leisure at home

## A  TV and music

I **watch TV** every night (*not* I ~~see~~ TV.)
I like **to watch** sports.   *or*   I like **watching** sports.
I **record** things on TV so I can watch them later.

I **listen to** music when I'm relaxing. (*not* I like to ~~hear~~ music ...)
I like to **download** different types of music.

## B  Hobbies / activities at home

Lots of kids / young people **play computer games**.
Do you surf **the Internet?** / Do you surf **the Web?**
Javier likes **cooking**.
Do you like **gardening**?
We **grow flowers** and **vegetables** in our garden.
I live in an apartment. I don't have a **garden**,
    but I have a lot of **house plants**.

## C  Reading

I **read** a lot at home.
What do you read?
Hattie reads **novels**. [long stories]
My Mom likes **books about** nature / different countries.
I like **magazines about** music, computers, and sports.
Do you read the (**news**)**paper** every day?

## D  Time with other people

Sometimes we **invite friends over** / **we have friends over for**
    **dinner** / **coffee** / **a party**. [We ask them to come to our home.]
I **call** my family every weekend. I like to **talk to** them.
I **text** my friends a lot.

## E  Just relaxing

Sometimes, I just **do nothing**.
I like to **hang out** [spend time with] with
    my friends and listen to music.
I like to **take a nap** [a short sleep, usually
    during the day] after lunch.

# Exercises

**56.1** What are these people doing?

1. She's ..................................................... .

4. She's ..................................................... .

2. He's ..................................................... .

5. She's ..................................................... .

3. He's ............................... the ............... .

6. He's .......................... to ..................... .

**56.2** Complete these sentences.

1. Sometimes I ........*listen*........ to CDs.
2. I ......................... to my sister on the phone every Sunday.
3. Some people like to ......................... a nap after lunch.
4. Do you ever ......................... friends over for dinner?
5. Some teenagers ......................... computer games at night.
6. Do you want to ......................... a movie tonight?
7. Did you ......................... the TV show about China yesterday?
8. My father ......................... vegetables in his garden.
9. Do you know how to ......................... things on TV to watch them later?

**56.3** Answer these questions about yourself.

1. If you have friends over, what do you like to do?
2. Do you like to download music? What kind?
3. What do you like to read?
4. How often do you text your friends?
5. What do you do when you hang out with your friends?
6. Do you have any plants in your room/apartment?

**56.4** Interesting or boring? Put these leisure activities in order, from *most interesting* to *most boring*, in your opinion.

| | | | |
|---|---|---|---|
| gardening | cooking | reading | surfing the Web |
| listening to music | doing nothing | watching TV | |

A crime is an action that is against the law. People who **commit** [do] serious crimes are called **criminals**.

**A** Crimes and criminals

**Stealing** means to take something that does not belong to you.
    Somebody **stole** my bicycle. (*not* Somebody ~~robbed~~ my bicycle.)
There are many ways to talk about **stealing**.

| *Crime* | *Criminal* |
|---|---|
| shoplifting [stealing from a store] | a shoplifter |
| theft [stealing things like cars or jewels] | a thief (a car or jewel thief) |
| burglary [stealing from a home] | a burglar |
| robbery [stealing from a person or a business] | a robber (a bank robber) |

The **shoplifter** had many CDs in her pocket. This was her second time **shoplifting** in that store.
The car **thief** was caught yesterday. He was responsible for the **theft** of 10 cars.
There was a **burglary** at the house down the street last night. **Burglars** took a TV and a computer.
There was a **robbery** at the main bank this morning. The **robber** was caught later this afternoon.

**B** The law

**The police arrested** a student **for** shoplifting this morning.
The student has to **go to court** next week.
If she is **guilty**, she will have to **pay a fine**.
If she is **innocent**, she can go home.
I don't think she will **go to prison**.

**C** Other crime problems

Some **vandals** [people who break and damage things] broke the store windows. We have a lot of **vandalism** in my city.

Computer **hackers** illegally take or change information on someone else's computer. **Hacking** can be dangerous.

If you **speed** [drive a car faster than the speed limit], you can get a ticket for **speeding** and have to pay a **fine**.

For some crimes people may have to do **community service**. [work in the community without pay]

# Exercises

**57.1**  **Name the criminal.**

1. A person who steals cars is a ..*car thief*........
2. Someone who walks into a bank and steals money is a ......................... .
3. A person who steals things from stores while pretending to shop is a ......................... .
4. Someone who enters people's houses and apartments to steal is a ......................... .
5. A person who steals jewels is a ......................... .

**57.2**  **Complete these sentences.**

1. The police officer ....*arrested*....... him for shoplifting.
2. Some v......................... destroyed all the flowers in the park.
3. The police stopped her for s......................... . She was doing 80 miles per hour (129 kilometers per hour) and the speed limit was 55 (89 kilometers per hour).
4. He had to pay a f......................... of $50 for parking his car in the wrong place.
5. The police made a mistake. She was i......................... . She did not steal the money.
6. There are a lot of b......................... in this part of the city, so always close the windows and lock the door.
7. A computer h......................... was sent to prison for stealing credit card information on the Internet.

**57.3**  **What do you think? Put these crimes in order from least serious to most serious.**

1. A student with no money stole a book from a bookstore.
2. A man was driving 90 miles per hour (145 kilometers per hour) and crashed his car, killing two people.
3. Five bank robbers robbed a bank during the day.
4. Vandals broke some lights in the park.
5. A rich woman shoplifted from a jewelry store.
6. Burglars entered a home, stealing a TV, cash, and some watches.
7. A man got 20 parking tickets.

**57.4**  **Choose five or six words from page 114 and use them to make your own sentences.**

115

## A TV and radio

**The news** [a report about important things that have happened recently] is on TV / on the radio at 6 o'clock every night. (*not* The news ~~are~~ on TV.)

Do you watch **soap operas / soaps**? [continuing dramatic stories about a group of people]

Do you like **reality shows** like *Survivor*?

I watch **game shows**.

I like **nature programs** best.

I watched a **documentary** [a program that gives information about a topic, based on facts] last night about immigration. [people coming to live in a different country]

On **talk shows**, famous people talk to a host about their lives.

I always watch **sports programs** and **movies** on TV.

The children watch **cartoons** [programs with drawings that move] on Saturday mornings. (See Unit 55 about movies.)

## B Newspapers and magazines

In some countries there are **morning newspapers** and **evening newspapers**.

Every week/month, I buy a **magazine**.

My mother buys **women's magazines**.

I like **news magazines** like *Newsweek* and *Time*.

My little brother buys **comics / comic books**. [magazines with stories told in pictures]

Other types of magazines: **sports magazines / computer magazines / teen magazines / fashion magazines** (See Unit 56 about leisure at home.)

## C Media and technology

Do you have **satellite TV**?

How many **channels** do you get? We get 200.

You can read some newspapers **on the Internet**.

satellite dish       computer

## D People and the media

There was **an interview with** the president on TV last night.

The people outside Brad Pitt's house are **reporters**. [people whose job is to discover information about news events and describe them for newspapers, TV, etc.]

My sister is **a journalist**. [person who writes news stories and articles for newspapers, magazines, TV, etc.] She writes for *The Valley* newspaper.

# Exercises

**58.1** **Complete the sentences with words from page 116.**

1. The news ..........*is*.......... on Channel 3 at 11 o'clock every night.
2. There was a ........................ about crime on TV last night.
3. Some people read ........................ magazines to get ideas about clothing.
4. I saw a ........................ program about birds in Antarctica.
5. My sister is 14. She reads ........................ magazines every week. She likes the love stories.
6. I can get the sports news on the ........................ with my computer.
7. Most children don't read newspapers. They look at pictures and read ........................ .

**58.2** **Match the description on the left with the TV show on the right.**

1. a movie star talks about his family life
2. show about people put on an island
3. soccer cup final
4. a person answer questions to win money
5. Maria decides to marry John (again)

    a. game show
    b. sports program
    c. soap opera
    d. reality show
    e. talk show

**58.3** **Put the articles in the box under the correct type of magazine.**

1. articles about health, diet, family
2. news about the Internet
3. articles about interesting women
4. pictures of pop musicians
5. interviews with the president
6. articles on the economy

| Computer magazines | Women's magazines | News magazines | Teen magazines |
|---|---|---|---|
| | | | |

**58.4** **Who or what is it?**

1. A person who discovers information and describes it for newspapers, TV, etc?
   *a reporter*
2. A person who writes articles in newspapers and magazines?
3. A newspaper you can buy every day after about 5 p.m.?
4. A magazine that children read, with cartoon pictures?
5. A TV program with factual information, sometimes analyzing problems in society?

**58.5** **Answer these questions about yourself.**

1. Do you read a morning or evening newspaper?
2. How many TV channels do you get?
3. How many hours of TV do you watch every day?
4. What are your favorite kinds of TV programs? What are your favorite radio shows?

# Everyday problems

## A  At home

The TV **isn't working**. Can you **fix** it?

The washing machine **is broken**. We need to **fix** it / **get it repaired**.

A: The plants are **dying**.
B: Did you forget to **water** them?

The room is **messy**. I have to **clean it up** / **clean up the room**.

**I lost** my keys. Will you help me **look for** them?

You **cut** your finger. You should
  **put on a Band-Aid**.

You **had an argument with** a friend. Will you **apologize**?
  [say "I'm sorry."]

## B  At work

Carla had a bad day at work yesterday. First, she was **late for** work.

She had **too much work to do**.
[more work than she could finish]

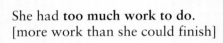

Her co-worker was **in a bad mood**.
[felt angry or sad]

Her **computer crashed**.
[The computer stopped working.]

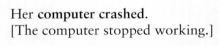 

The (photo)copier was **out of order**.

The coffeemaker **wasn't working**.

 **tip**  *When you need to make a list of things to do, make it in English,
e.g., Fix my bike. Water the plants. Clean up my desk.*

# Exercises

**59.1** Look at the pictures. What is the problem?

1. *The coffeemaker isn't working.*
2. ..........................................................................................................................
3. ..........................................................................................................................
4. ..........................................................................................................................
5. ..........................................................................................................................
6. ..........................................................................................................................
7. ..........................................................................................................................
8. ..........................................................................................................................

**59.2** Choose three nouns from the box that can go with these words.

| cup   finger   room   knees   camera   an appointment |
| --- |
| hair dryer   radio   hair   washing machine   glass   desk |
| window   TV   hand   class   computer   work |

1. broken *window/cup/glass* ...................
2. cut ....................................................
3. messy ................................................
4. late for ...........................................
5. a ................................................ that isn't working
6. fix a ................................................

**59.3** Which of these would be big problems for you? Which would be small problems? Write your opinion after each problem.

1. a TV that doesn't work – *small problem*
2. dying plants
3. a cut finger
4. late for work
5. a co-worker in a bad mood
6. a photocopier that is out of order
7. a coffeemaker that isn't working
8. a broken washing machine
9. a messy bedroom
10. an argument with a friend
11. a computer crash
12. lost keys
13. too much work

**59.4.** Look at Carla's problems in B on page 118. What could she do?

*She was late for work – leave home earlier next time.*

**59.5.** Can you think of three everyday problems that you or people you know have had recently? Write them down in English. Use a dictionary if you need help.

## A  Natural disasters

There was a **hurricane / snowstorm / forest fire** last year.
**hurricane** [extremely strong winds that can cause great damage]
**snowstorm** [a storm with a lot of snow and strong winds at the same time]
**forest fire** [Trees catch fire and fire spreads quickly, often when it is very dry.]
California has had a lot of **earthquakes**. [The earth moves.]
After the heavy rains, **floods** [Water covers an area that is usually dry.] severely
  damaged the town.

hurricane          snowstorm          forest fire

## B  Problems caused by people

There are too many people in some places. Cities are too crowded. Some people
cannot find jobs and are **unemployed**. Some people cannot find a place to live and
are **homeless**.

Many people in cities are **poor**.  [They do not have enough money.] Without money,
many people are also **hungry**. [They do not have enough food.]

There is a lot of **pollution** in many cities. [The air, water, or earth is dirty and
harmful to people, plants, and animals, especially because of chemicals or waste.]
The **air pollution** is very bad today.
The river is **polluted**, and a lot of fish have died.

Several countries are now at **war**. [fighting between two or more countries or
nationalities]

The **traffic jams** [when there are too many cars
on the road, moving very slowly] in the city are
terrible **during (the) rush hour**. [times when
everyone is going to work or coming home]

There was an **accident** on the freeway. [One or more cars hit something or hit each
other.]

There's a teachers' **strike** today. [They will not work because of a disagreement.]
The bus drivers are **on strike**.

> **tip**   *Try to listen to or read the news in English on the Internet every day.*

# Exercises

**60.1** What problems can you see in the pictures?

1. ......*strike*...............

4. ...................................

7. ...................................

2. ...................................

5. ...................................

8. ...................................

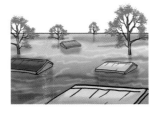

3. ...................................

6. ...................................

9. ...................................

**60.2** Write down all the problems from page 120 that you have in your country and the places where you have them.

*earthquakes – in the mountains*
*traffic jams – in the big cities*

**60.3** Complete the sentences with words from page 120.

1. Cars make air .....*pollution*..... worse in cities.
2. Their wages were very low, so the workers went on ......................................... .
3. My grandfather was a soldier in the Second World ......................................... .
4. Sue had an ......................................... last year, but fortunately no one was hurt.
5. Japan often has ...................................., and Siberia often has .................................... .
6. When people are ........................................., they sometimes sleep on the streets.
7. Some cities have special programs to help the ......................................... find jobs.
8. Many people take trains or buses to avoid ......................................... traffic.

# Common weights and measures

## Linear measures

| | | |
|---|---|---|
| 1 foot | = | 12 inches |
| 1 yard | = | 36 inches |
| 1 mile | = | 5,280 feet |

| | | |
|---|---|---|
| 10 millimeters | = | 1 centimeter |
| 100 centimeters | = | 1 meter |
| 1,000 meters | = | 1 kilometer |

| | | |
|---|---|---|
| 1.6 kilometers | = | 1 mile |

## Weight

| | | |
|---|---|---|
| 1 pound | = | 16 ounces |
| 1 ton | = | 2,000 pounds |

| | | |
|---|---|---|
| 1,000 milligrams | = | 1 gram |
| 1,000 grams | = | 1 kilogram |
| 1,000 kilograms | = | 1 metric ton |

| | | |
|---|---|---|
| 1 kilogram | = | 2.2 pounds |

## Liquid volume measures

| | | | | |
|---|---|---|---|---|
| 1 tablespoon | = | 3 teaspoons | | |
| 1 fluid ounce | = | 2 tablespoons | | |
| 1 cup | = | 8 fluid ounces | | |
| 1 pint | = | 16 fluid ounces | = | 2 cups |
| 1 quart | = | 32 fluid ounces | = | 2 pints |
| 1 gallon | = | 128 fluid ounces | = | 4 quarts |
| 1 barrel | = | 31.5 gallons | | |

| | | |
|---|---|---|
| 10 milliliters | = | 1 centiliter |
| 1,000 milliliters | = | 1 liter |

| | | |
|---|---|---|
| 1 liter | = | 2.1 pints |

## Temperature

| | | | | |
|---|---|---|---|---|
| -18 degrees Celsius (C) | = | 0 | degrees Fahrenheit (F) | |
| 0 degrees C | = | 32 | degrees F | Freezing point of water |
| 37 degrees C | = | 98.6 | degrees F | Normal human body temperature |
| 100 degrees C | = | 212 | degrees F | Boiling point of water |

# Phonetic symbols

## Vowel sounds

| Symbol | Examples | Symbol | Examples |
|---|---|---|---|
| /ɑ/ | h<u>o</u>t, <u>fa</u>ther, s<u>o</u>ck, st<u>ar</u> | /ɔ:/ | s<u>aw</u>, th<u>ough</u>t, b<u>a</u>ll |
| /æ/ | h<u>a</u>t, l<u>a</u>st, b<u>a</u>g | /ɔɪ/ | b<u>oy</u>, j<u>oi</u>n |
| /ɑɪ/ | b<u>i</u>te, r<u>i</u>de, sk<u>y</u>, h<u>eigh</u>t | /oʊ/ | g<u>o</u>, b<u>oa</u>t, bel<u>ow</u> |
| /ɑʊ/ | h<u>ou</u>se, n<u>ow</u> | /ʊ/ | p<u>u</u>t, g<u>oo</u>d |
| /e/ | l<u>e</u>t, h<u>ea</u>d, s<u>ai</u>d; *before* /r/: f<u>air</u>, r<u>a</u>re | /u:/ | f<u>oo</u>d, bl<u>ue</u>, sh<u>oe</u>, l<u>o</u>se |
| /eɪ/ | l<u>a</u>te, n<u>a</u>me, s<u>ay</u> | /ʌ/ | *stressed*: s<u>u</u>n, l<u>o</u>ve, <u>u</u>nder |
| /i:/ | sl<u>ee</u>p, m<u>e</u>, happ<u>y</u> | /ə/ | *unstressed*: <u>a</u>lone, lab<u>e</u>l, c<u>o</u>llect, und<u>e</u>r |
| /ɪ/ | f<u>i</u>t, p<u>i</u>n, <u>i</u>f | /ɜ/ | *before* /r/: b<u>ir</u>d, t<u>ur</u>n, earn |

## Consonant sounds

| Symbol | Examples | Symbol | Examples |
|---|---|---|---|
| /b/ | <u>b</u>id, ro<u>b</u> | /s/ | <u>s</u>ee, mou<u>s</u>e, re<u>c</u>ent |
| /d/ | <u>d</u>id, un<u>d</u>er | /ʃ/ | <u>sh</u>oe, ca<u>sh</u>, na<u>ti</u>on |
| /ð/ | <u>th</u>is, mo<u>th</u>er, brea<u>the</u> | /t/ | <u>t</u>eam, mee<u>t</u>, ma<u>tt</u>er, sen<u>t</u> |
| /dʒ/ | <u>j</u>udge <u>g</u>entle | /tʃ/ | <u>ch</u>urch, ri<u>ch</u>, ca<u>tch</u> |
| /f/ | <u>f</u>oot, sa<u>f</u>e, lau<u>gh</u> | /θ/ | <u>th</u>ink, bo<u>th</u> |
| /g/ | <u>g</u>o, ru<u>g</u>, bi<u>gg</u>er | /v/ | <u>v</u>isit, sa<u>v</u>e |
| /h/ | <u>h</u>ouse, be<u>h</u>ind, <u>wh</u>ole | /w/ | <u>w</u>atch, a<u>w</u>ay, <u>w</u>ear; <u>wh</u>ich, <u>wh</u>ere – *Many North American speakers pronounce /w/ in such words and many pronounced* /hw/. |
| /j/ | <u>y</u>es, <u>u</u>seful, m<u>u</u>sic | | |
| /k/ | <u>k</u>ick, <u>c</u>ook, qui<u>ck</u> | | |
| /l/ | <u>l</u>ook, ba<u>ll</u>, fee<u>l</u>, poo<u>l</u> | | |
| /m/ | <u>m</u>any, so<u>m</u>e, da<u>m</u>p | /z/ | <u>z</u>oo, ha<u>s</u>, the<u>s</u>e |
| /n/ | <u>n</u>one, su<u>nn</u>y, se<u>n</u>t | /ʒ/ | mea<u>s</u>ure, bei<u>g</u>e, A<u>s</u>ia |
| /ŋ/ | ri<u>ng</u>, thi<u>n</u>k, lo<u>ng</u>er | | |
| /p/ | <u>p</u>eel, soa<u>p</u>, <u>p</u>e<u>pp</u>er | | |
| /r/ | <u>r</u>ead, ca<u>rr</u>y, fa<u>r</u>, ca<u>r</u>d – *In some parts of North America* /r/ *is not always pronounced at the ends of words or before consonants.* | | |

# List of irregular verbs

## B

| | | |
|---|---|---|
| be (am/is/are) | was/were | been |
| beat | beat | beaten |
| become | became | become |
| begin | began | begun |
| bend | bent | bent |
| bet | bet | bet |
| bite | bit | bitten |
| blow | blew | blown |
| break | broke | broken |
| bring | brought | brought |
| build | built | built |
| burst | burst | burst |
| buy | bought | bought |

## C

| | | |
|---|---|---|
| catch | caught | caught |
| choose | chose | chosen |
| come | came | come |
| cost | cost | cost |
| cut | cut | cut |

## D

| | | |
|---|---|---|
| dig | dug | dug |
| do | did | done |
| draw | drew | drawn |
| drink | drank | drunk |
| drive | drove | driven |

## E

| | | |
|---|---|---|
| eat | ate | eaten |

## F

| | | |
|---|---|---|
| fall | fell | fallen |
| feed | fed | fed |
| feel | felt | felt |
| fight | fought | fought |
| find | found | found |
| fit | fit | fit |
| fly | flew | flown |
| forget | forgot | forgotten |
| freeze | froze | frozen |

## G

| | | |
|---|---|---|
| get | got | gotten |
| give | gave | given |
| go | went | gone |
| grow | grew | grown |

## H

| | | |
|---|---|---|
| hang | hung | hung |
| have | had | had |
| hear | heard | heard |
| hide | hid | hidden |
| hit | hit | hit |
| hold | held | held |
| hurt | hurt | hurt |

## K

| | | |
|---|---|---|
| keep | kept | kept |
| know | knew | known |

## L

| | | |
|---|---|---|
| lead | led | led |
| leave | left | left |
| lend | lent | lent |
| let | let | let |
| lose | lost | lost |

## M

| | | |
|---|---|---|
| make | made | made |
| mean | meant | meant |
| meet | met | met |

**P**

| | | |
|---|---|---|
| pay | paid | paid |
| put | put | put |

**Q**

| | | |
|---|---|---|
| quit | quit | quit |

**R**

| | | |
|---|---|---|
| read | read | read |
| ride | rode | ridden |
| ring | rang | rung |
| rise | rose | risen |
| run | ran | run |

**S**

| | | |
|---|---|---|
| say | said | said |
| see | saw | seen |
| sell | sold | sold |
| send | sent | sent |
| shake | shook | shaken |
| shine | shone | shone |
| shoot | shot | shot |
| show | showed | shown |
| shut | shut | shut |
| sing | sang | sung |
| sink | sank | sunk |
| sit | sat | sat |
| sleep | slept | slept |
| speak | spoke | spoken |
| spend | spent | spent |
| spread | spread | spread |
| stand | stood | stood |
| steal | stole | stolen |
| sweep | swept | swept |
| swim | swam | swum |

**T**

| | | |
|---|---|---|
| take | took | taken |
| teach | taught | taught |
| tear | tore | torn |
| tell | told | told |
| think | thought | thought |
| throw | threw | thrown |

**U**

| | | |
|---|---|---|
| understand | understood | understood |

**W**

| | | |
|---|---|---|
| wake | woke | woken |
| wear | wore | worn |
| win | won | won |
| write | wrote | written |

# Index

## Unit 1

adjective
blank
bus
capital letter
children
clothes
column
complete
concept
correct
follow
grammar
group
instructions
man
match
noun
paragraph
phrase
plural
preposition
question
sentence
singular
speak
topic
verb
woman

## Unit 2

big
bottle
bread
clothes
collocation
cool
cup
diagram
door
drink
dry
eat
education
exercise

fork
furniture
glass
happy
headlight
high
knife
learn
light
milk
mistake
notebook
picture
rainy
rice
salad
school
spoon
strategy
student
teacher
test
tire
tire (car)
travel
trunk
warm
water
wet
window
windshield

## Unit 3

baby
breakfast
brother
class
coffee
cold
computer
course
exam
have
house
money

museum
must
necessary
own
party
possess
problem
restaurant
sick
sister
tea
thirsty
trip
weekend

## Unit 4

aunt
downtown
go
go dancing
go fishing
go shopping
go sightseeing
go skiing
go swimming
hill
movies
stairs
summer
vacation
where
winter

## Unit 5

boy
company
do business with
do homework
do the cooking
do the dishes
do the housework
do the laundry
doctor

engineer
girl
kitchen
lawyer
man
microwave
music
relax
secretary
student
woman

## Unit 6

clothes
dentist
dinner
dirty
doctor
homework
make a call
make a copy
make a decision
make a meal
make a mistake
make a video
make an appointment
make breakfast
make coffee
make dinner
make lunch
make me feel angry
make me feel nervous
make me feel sad
nice
say
waiter
welcome

## Unit 7

ATM machine
barbecue
candy
come
come back
come in
come on
come out
come over

door
here
how come
knock
late
miss
opposite
pizza
return
review
someone
there
yesterday

## Unit 8

airport
allergy
art
camera
cold
country
course
foreign
health
history
language
medicine
rain
semester
Spanish
subway
summer
sunscreen
take
take a nap
take a picture
take a shower
take time
taxi
tired
umbrella
weekend
yoga

## Unit 9

advise
book
borrow

brother
CD
chocolate
e-mail address
example
flower
give
give a call
give a message
give advice
give an explanation
give back
give directions
give me a break
give me a hand
give money
give permission
give up
library
permit
phrasal verb
please
pronoun
receive
sports club

## Unit 10

earn
fruit
get
get a haircut
get back
get cold
get dark
get home
get light
get married
get ready
get there
get tired
get to
get wet
mail
postcard
storm
sun
university
window

## Unit 11

alarm clock
beach
children
coat
come on
come up
get along
get up
give up
go off
go on
happen
job
leave
loud
music
news
phrasal verb
plane
put on
refuse
remove
snow
stop
subject
swimsuit
take off
turn down
turn off
turn on
turn up
underline
uniform

## Unit 12

bus
call a friend
check e-mail
clean the house
come home
do the laundry
drive
everyday
get up
go for a walk
go to sleep
go to work
have breakfast

how often
listen to music
make dinner
normally
sometimes
surf the Internet
take a shower
toast
train
usually
wake up
walk
watch TV
weekend
what time
work

## Unit 13

answer
ask
ask someone a question
ask someone for something
ask someone for the time
ask someone to do some-
    thing
Chinese
congratulations
goodbye
happy birthday
happy new year
hello
Japanese
Malay
please
police officer
Portuguese
say
speak
subway
talk
tell
tell someone a joke
tell someone a phone
    number
tell someone a story
tell someone the time
tell someone your age
tell someone your e-mail
    address
tell someone your name
thank you

## Unit 14

airline
arrive at
arrive in
break
carry
catch
climb
dance
drive
elephant
fall
fly
jog
jump
miss
morning
mountain
movement
pass
pool
pull
push
race
rain
ride
run
swim
table
take
transportation
truck
walk

## Unit 15

after
agree
also
although
and
as well
because
before
business
but
circle
conjunction
connecting word
even

family
father
function
graduate
grandmother
if
job
like
love
marry
mother
move
only
rock star
so
son
tennis
than
too
when

## Unit 16

abbreviation
afternoon
April
August
autumn
century
day
day after tomorrow
day before yesterday
December
evening
fall *(n)* season
fall *(v)*
February
Friday
hour
January
July
June
March
May
minute
mistake
Monday
month
morning
noon
November

October
Saturday
season
September
spring
summer
Sunday
Thursday
time
today
tomorrow
Tuesday
Wednesday
week
weekend
winter
year
yesterday

## Unit 17

always
four times a year
future
hardly ever
hat
in a minute
in the future
in the past
last
last year
later
never
next
next year
now
o'clock
often
once a week
past
present
recently
right now
soccer
sometimes
then
three or four times a month
twice a day
usually

## Unit 18

away
back
beginning
bottom
end
everywhere
front
here
home
left
middle
out
out of town
overseas
right
side
study
there
top

## Unit 19

bad
badly
dangerous
difficulty
easily
fast
loud
loudly
normal
poor
poorly
quick
quickly
quiet
quietly
right
sadly
safely
slow
slowly
soft
softly
strangely
suddenly
unhappy
well
wrong

## Unit 20

be
become
begin
break
bring
buy
catch
choose
come
cost
cut
do
drink
drive
eat
fall
feel
fight
find
fly
forget
get
give
go
have
hear
hurt
keep
know
leave
let
lose
make
meet
pay
play
put
read
ride
ring
run
say
see
sell
send
shoot
shut
sing
sink
sit

sleep
speak
spend
stand
steal
swim
take
teach
tear
tell
think
throw
understand
wake
wear
win
write

## Unit 21

advice
air
apples
baggage
beef
bread
butter
countable
furniture
homework
information
luggage
milk
news
plates
rice
shoes
spaghetti
sugar
traffic
travel
uncountable
water
weather
work

## Unit 22

awesome
awful
bad

beautiful
best
better
excellent
fantastic
fine
good
gorgeous
great
horrible
jacket
keys
mean
nasty
nice
perfect
super
terrible
terrific
wonderful
worse
worst

## Unit 23

childish
difficult
friendly
great
happy
intelligent
kind
mean
nice
selfish
smart
stupid
terrific
thoughtful
well behaved
wonderful

## Unit 24

afraid of
apologize for
ask for
bad at
belong to
good at

130

interested in
listen to
look at
look for
look forward to
look up
math
mice
pay for
science
sports
thank someone for
think about
wait for

## Unit 25

divorced
ex-boss
ex-boyfriend
ex-wife
impolite
impossible
incomplete
inconsiderate
inconvenient
incorrect
informal
misbehave
misjudge
misspell
misunderstand
nonfat
nonresident
nonsmoking
prepaid
preschool
redo
regular
repaint
reread
retell
rewrite
talks
unanswered
uncomfortable
unfinished
unfriendly
unhappy
unsafe
unsure

## Unit 26

badly
beach
beautiful
biology
book
calculator
can opener
car
cloudy
economics
endless
happily
happiness
harder
hopeful
idea
instructor
loneliness
mathematics
painless
picture
politics
psychology
quickly
rainy
sadness
sandy
slowly
smile
sociology
stapler
sunny
surfer
swimmer
useful
useless
weather

## Unit 27

bless you
congratulations
excuse me
fine, thanks
good afternoon
good evening
good morning
good night
goodbye
happy birthday

happy new year
have a nice day
hello
hi
how are you
I'm sorry
please
pretty good
see you later
sleep well
take care
thank you
thanks
you're welcome

## Unit 28

apartment
be used to
bedtime
chase
concert
fire alarm
hear
its
it's
listen
look
look at
newspaper
painting
see
sign
story
street
their
they're
used to
vocabulary
watch
your
you're

## Unit 29

birthday
born
bride
bridegroom
ceremony

dead
death
die
funeral
grandfather
grandmother
grandparents
heart attack
honeymoon
legally
marriage
married
name
religious
shock
single
widow
widower

## Unit 30

aunt
brother
cousin
daughter
family tree
father
granddaughter
grandfather
grandmother
grandson
mother
nephew
niece
parent
relative
sister
son
uncle
wife

## Unit 31

arm
back
blood
brain
chest
ear
eye

feet
fingernail
foot
hair
hand
heart
hip
knee
leg
lip
mouth
neck
nose
shoulder
skin
stomach
teeth
thumb
toe
tooth
waist

## Unit 32

belt
boots
carry
coat
dress
get dressed
get undressed
glasses
gloves
hat
jacket
jeans
(neck)tie
pants
put on
scarf
shirt
shoes
shorts
skirt
socks
suit
sunglasses
sweater
take off
T-shirt
wear

## Unit 33

average
beard
beautiful
black
blonde
blue
brown
dark
elderly
fair
fat
feet
green
handsome
height
how much do you weigh
how tall
inch
large
light
long
meter
middle-aged
mustache
old
ordinary-looking
overweight
pretty
short
slim
tall
thin
ugly
unattractive
young

## Unit 34

allergy
aspirin
asthma
better
cancer
cold
cough
cough syrup
dentist
diet
exercise

fine
flower
get some exercise
grass
headache
in the hospital
OK
pollution
relax
serious
sick
sneeze
stress
throw up
toothache
traffic fumes
very well
vomit

## Unit 35

angry
cat
chocolate
cold
cooking
dancing
dislike
driving
happy
hate
horror movie
hot
hungry
jazz
like
love
sad
sick
soccer
surprised
thirsty
tired
traffic
upset
warm

## Unit 36

Africa
Asia

Australia
Australian
Brazilian
British
Canadian
Chilean
Chinese
continent
country
Danish
Dutch
Egyptian
Europe
Filipino
France
French
Greek
Holland
Indonesian
Iraqi
Irish
Israeli
Italian
Japanese
Korean
language
Mexican
North America
people
Peruvian
Philippines
Polish
Portuguese
Russian
Senegalese
South America
Spanish
Swedish
Swiss
Switzerland
Thai
Turkish
Venuzuelan
Vietnamese

## Unit 37

Celsius
cloud
cloudy
dangerous

degree
extremely
Fahrenheit
favorite
fog
foggy
forecast
hurricane
lightning
minus
rain
season
snow
snowy
storm
sun
sunny
thunder
thunderstorm
weather
wind

## Unit 38

bank
bank teller
borrow books
bus stop
can I
change money
check e-mail
city
city hall
downtown
excuse me, I'm looking for
get a train
how do I get to
is there
librarian
museum
no entry
no parking
park your car
parking garage
parking lot
pay phone
police officer
railroad crossing
salesclerk
signal ahead
take a train

taxi driver
train station
where's

## Unit 39

animal
bird
cabin
country
countryside
enviroment
farm
fields
forest
hills
lake
mountains
natural
nature
path
plant
river
road
simple
town
tractor
trail
wildlife
woods

## Unit 40

animal
bacon
beef
calf
cat
chick
chicken
cow
dog
egg
elephant
farm
fish
giraffe
ham
lamb
leather

lion
milk
monkey
mutton
parakeet
parrot
pet
pig
piglet
pork
sheep
snake
take for a walk
tiger
turtle
veal
wool
zoo

## Unit 41

airplane
baggage claim
bicycle
bike
boarding pass
boat
bus
car
carry-on luggage
change trains
check in
check your luggage
confirmation number
customs
depart
dining car
fill up with gas
flight
helicopter
land
leave
luggage
map
motorcycle
one-way
passport
plane
platform
rent a car
ride

round-trip
schedule
ship
subway
take off
taxi
train
transportation
travel

## Unit 42

cashier
caution
closed
gentlemen
go in
go out
keep off the grass
ladies
men
notice
open
out of order
pay here
pull
push
restroom
sale
sign
warning
women

## Unit 43

apple
banana
bread
cake
carrot
coffee
dessert
drink
everyday
fish
food
French fries
garlic
grape
green bean

hamburger
hot dog
ice cream
juice
junk food
meat
milk
mineral water
mushroom
onion
orange
pasta
pea
pear
pineapple
pizza
pop
potato
rice
soda
sparkling water
strawberry
tea
tomato

## Unit 44

bowl
cabinet
can I help with
chopsticks
coffeemaker
counter
cupboard
dish
dish detergent
dish soap
dishtowel
dishwasher
faucet
fork
freezer
frying pan
glass
kitchen
knife
microwave
mug
oven
paper towel
plate

pot
refrigerator
saucer
sink
spoon
stove
teapot
where does this
where can I find
where should I put

## Unit 45

alarm clock
bathtub
bathroom
bedroom
brush your teeth
closet
comb
dresser
eat breakfast
fall asleep
get dressed
get into bed
get undressed
get up
go to bed
go to the bathroom
hairbrush
have a wash
medicine cabinet
mirror
night table
nightgown
nightstand
pajamas
pillow
shampoo
shelf
shower
sink
soap
table lamp
take a shower
toilet
toilet paper
toothbrush
toothpaste
towel
wake up

## Unit 46

against
armchair
book
bookcase
carpet
chair
close the curtains
coffee table
curtain
couch
drape
electrical outlet
end table
in the corner
in the middle of
light switch
listen to music
living room
near
next to
phone
phone book
picture
read
reading lamp
relax
remote control
sofa
stereo
television
turn on the light
turn on the TV
TV
under
watch TV

## Unit 47

college
court
doctor
factory
farm
farmer
garage
hair salon
hairdresser
hospital
job

lawyer
mechanic
nurse
office
receptionist
salesclerk
school
store
teacher
waiter
waitress

## Unit 48

art
biology
business
chalkboard
chemistry
computer science
desk
English
eraser
fail a test
fail an exam
geography
get a degree
graduate
history
homework
languages
laptop computer
lecture
mathematics
music
notebook
paper clip
pass a test
pass an exam
pen
pencil sharpener
physics
piece of paper
ruler
school
stapler
subject
take a course
take a test
take an exam
take notes
textbook

## Unit 49

call
can I take a message
cell phone
communication
e-mail address
envelope
fax
fax machine
fax number
government
office
pay phone
phone number
professor
stamp
subject
text
text message

## Unit 50

camera
credit card
drive
guidebook
have a good time
local currency
local food
luggage
nightlife
passport
plane
postcard
take the bus
take the ferry
take the train
ticket
tourist information center /
    office
trip
visa

## Unit 51

aspirin
bag
bakery
basement
beach ball

bookstore
bread
cash
cash register
cashier
change
check book
clothes
coins
cost
credit card
department store
different color
drugstore
DVD player
electronics store
furniture
gift shop
grocery store
hammer
hardware store
larger size
lipstick
makeup
MP3 player
pay by check
post office
postcard
receipt
shopping
skin care product
skirt
smaller size
stationery
supermarket
toy store
try it on
use a credit card

## Unit 52

bathroom
bathtub
bill
check in
coffeemaker
concierge
confirmation number
double room
dry-cleaning
elevator

fill out
form
front desk
hair dryer
hotel
Internet connection
luggage
ninth floor
nonsmoking
phone
reception desk
reservation
room key
room service
shower
sign
single room
TV
valet parking
wake-up call
Wi-Fi

## Unit 53

appetizer
baked
beverage
café
coffee shop
cola
deli
dessert
eat out
entrée
fast-food restaurant
iced
included
main course
mashed
meal
medium
menu
order
pop
rare
restaurant
romantic
salad
sandwich
service
shrimp cocktail

snack
soda
soft drink
soup
steak
tip
vegetarian option
well-done

## Unit 54

ball game
baseball
basketball
bowl
bowling
bowling alley
court
cycling
exercise
field
football
golf
ice skating
judo
karate
Ping-Pong
play
rink
run
running
sailing
skiing
soccer
sport
swimming
swimming pool
table tennis
tennis
volleyball

## Unit 55

action movie
animated film
boring
cartoon
comedy
cowboy
detective movie

director
go to the movies
horror movie
love story
movie
movie star
musical
romantic comedy
romantic movie
science fiction movie
thriller
watch a movie
Western

## Unit 56

call
cooking
do nothing
garden
gardening
grow flowers
grow vegetables
hang out
have friends over
house plant
Internet
invite friends over
leisure
listen to music
magazine
newspaper
novel
play computer games
record
take a nap
talk
text
watch
Web

## Unit 57

arrest
burglar
burglary
commit
community service
crime
criminal

fine
go to court
go to prison
guilty
hacker
hacking
innocent
parking ticket
pay a fine
police
robber
robbery
shoplifter
shoplifting
speed
steal
theft
thief
vandal
vandalism

## Unit 58

article
cartoon
channel
comic
documentary
economy
fashion
game show
interview
journalist
magazine

media
musician
nature program
news
newspaper
politician
radio show
reality show
reporter
satellite TV
soap opera
sports program
talk show
teen

## Unit 59

apologize
Band-Aid
broken
clean up
coworker
crash
cut
die
fix
get repaired
have an argument
in a bad mood
late for
look for
lose
messy
out of order

problem
too much work to do
washing machine
water
work

## Unit 60

accident
air pollution
crowded
during the rush hour
earthquake
flood
forest fire
global
homeless
hungry
hurricane
natural disaster
on strike
polluted
pollution
poor
problem
snowstorm
soldier
strike
traffic jam
unemployed
wages
war

# Answer key

## Unit 1

**1.1**

| Noun | Verb | Adjective | Adverb | Preposition |
|------|------|-----------|--------|-------------|
| shirt | speak | bad | quietly | of |
| car | write | new | quickly | by |
| banana | eat | old | daily | at |
| woman | go | sad | correctly | in |

**1.2**
2. question
3. phrase
4. sentence
5. question
6. sentence

**1.3**
2. woman
3. No, it's a preposition.
4. No, it's a noun.
5. No, it's a sentence.

**1.4**
1. is
*Possible answers:*
2. I have brown / dark brown / blue / green eyes.
3. speak; English; He has seven cats.
4. make a mistake; do homework; take a shower
5.

| Food | Clothes |
|------|---------|
| rice | hat |
| milk | coat |

## Unit 2

**2.1** *Possible answers:*
have a class; have a cup of coffee; have a meeting

**2.2**
wet
dry
warm — weather
cool
rainy

**2.3**

| Name of word family | Words in family |
|---------------------|-----------------|
| education | school, teacher, notebook, test, student |
| food | bread, milk, water, salad, rice |

**2.4**  *Possible pictures:*

1. a plane **lands**   2. **sunny** weather   3. **under** the table

**2.5**  *Possible words:*

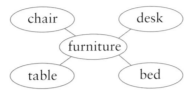

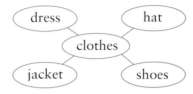

## Unit 3

**3.1**  *Possible answers:*
2. appointment   4. party   6. cold   8. baby
3. test   5. time   7. date

**3.2**  *Possible answers:*
1. Yes, I have two brothers and a sister.
2. I have classes on Mondays and Wednesdays.   *or*   I don't have any classes.
3. I usually have a sandwich or a salad.
4. I don't have to get up early on weekends.   *or*   On weekends I have to get up early to go to work.   *or*   I like to get up early on weekends, but I don't have to.
5. I usually have coffee with breakfast.
6. I want a new computer.
7. Sometimes I have trouble understanding English when people talk very fast.
8. I have to study hard, but I enjoy learning.

**3.3**

|   |   |   |   |   |
|---|---|---|---|---|
| ¹M | ²E | A | L |   |
|   | X |   |   |   |
| ³P | A | R | ⁴T | Y |
|   | M | ■ | E |   |
|   | ⁵S | N | A | C | K |

**3.4**  *Possible answers:*
1. Why don't you have something to drink / have a drink / have a cup of coffee / have a cup of tea?
2. Do you have a cold?
3. Bye, have a good trip!
4. I can't, I have a big test on Monday and I have to study this weekend.

## Unit 4

**4.1**  2. Jean and Mike are going to the mall. They are going to go shopping.
3. Antonio is going to Rome.  He's going to go sightseeing.

4. The Lees are going to the beach. They are going to go swimming.
5. Sun-hee is going to the lake. She is going to go fishing.

4.2
2. We're going sightseeing today.
3. Joe went up to the top of the hill.   *or*   Joe went down to the bottom of the hill.
4. Where does this bus go?
5. Sarah went out to dinner.

4.3
2. On Tuesday Sue is going to write to Luis.
3. On Wednesday she is going to watch the World Cup on TV.
4. On Thursday she is going to meet David.
5. On Friday she is going to go to the movies.

4.4
*Possible answers:*
I sometimes go swimming. I never go skiing.
I sometimes go dancing. I never go fishing.
I always go sightseeing.

## Unit 5

5.1
2. She's doing the cooking.
3. They're doing their homework.
4. They're doing the laundry.
5. He's doing his exercises.

5.2
2. What does Bill Atkins do? He's a teacher.
3. What does Maria Santos do? She's a doctor.
4. What do Ted and Kumiko do? They're students.

5.3
*Possible answers:*
2. No, they don't.
3. Yes, I do.
4. No, I didn't
5. Yes, it does.
6. No, I didn't.

5.4
*Possible answers:*
I usually do the dishes.
My husband and I both do the laundry.
My wife does business with Argentina.
I hate doing the housework.
I love doing the cooking.
My mother always does a good job.

## Unit 6

6.1
2. do        3. make        4. makes        5. do

6.2
1. That movie made/makes me sad.   *or*   That movie made/makes me feel sad.
2. Tests at school always make/made me nervous.   *or*   Tests at school always make/made me feel nervous.
3. The waiter wasn't very nice to me. It made/makes me angry.   *or*   … It made/makes me feel angry.
4. You were so nice to me. You made/make me (feel) very welcome.

**6.3**
1. She's making a copy.
2. She's making tea.
3. He's making a phone call / a telephone call.
4. They're making a video / a movie.

**6.4**
2. Can I **take** a picture of you?
3. He's 35, but he never **does** his own laundry. He takes his dirty clothes to his mother's.
4. I have to **make** an appointment with the dentist.
5. Do students have to **take** a test at the end of their English course?
6. We have to **make** a decision today.

## Unit 7

**7.1**
2. Come; go     4. in      6. over
3. back         5. come    7. on

**7.2**  *Possible answers:*
1. Come in!
2. We're going to have a barbecue tomorrow. Do you want to come (over)?

**7.3**
1. Come      3. comes     5. came
2. came      4. come

## Unit 8

**8.1**
1. takes the train; takes          3. take a taxi/cab; takes
2. takes the school bus / the bus  4. take the subway

**8.2**
1. taking any classes    3. take a test
2. took a course         4. took yoga lessons

**8.3**  *Possible answers:*
2. I take a shower.      4. I take medicine.
3. I take my passport.   5. I take a nap.

**8.4**  *Possible answer:*
It took me about an hour to do this unit.

## Unit 9

**9.1**
2. Tony gave his mom a box of chocolates for her birthday.
3. Grandmother / His grandmother gave Andy a camera for his birthday.
4. Sam gave Anna some flowers for her birthday.

**9.2**
2. She gave it to Andy.
3. He gave them to his mom/mother.
4. He gave them to Anna.

**9.3**
2. Give me a call on Saturday.
3. Please give me advice.
4. They'll never give you permission to take so many books out of the library.
5. When you e-mail Maria don't forget to give her a (good) explanation why you can't go to her party.

**9.4**
1. money      4. examples
2. number     5. e-mail address
3. message

**9.5**  1. give me a hand      4. give … back
        2. give up            5. Give me a break!
        3. give … away

**Unit 10**

**10.1**  *Possible answers:*
        2. it's getting light.      4. I'm getting wet!
        3. He's getting ready.      5. I'm getting cold.

**10.2**  *Possible answers:*
        2. I get a job.                    4. I get a haircut.
        3. I get a pen/pencil and paper.   5. I get a cup of coffee/tea.

**10.3**  *Possible answers:*
        2. It takes 25 minutes to get to my house from the university.
        3. He got a haircut.
        4. He is getting ready (for school).
        5. It got dark.

**10.4**  *Possible answers:*
        1. In the U.S. and Canada, many people get married when they are 20 to 30
           years old.
        2. People usually get married on weekends, often on Saturday. The summer
           months (June, July, and August) are very popular.
        3. I get home at about 6 o'clock.
        4. I get there / I get home on the bus.

**Unit 11**

**11.1**  2. e      3. b      4. d      5. a

**11.2**  2. off        6. along
        3. on; up     7. up
        4. off        8. on
        5. off

**11.3**  2. The alarm clock is going off.
        3. The boy is getting up.
        4. The woman is turning on the oven.

**11.4**  2. going on       5. got up
        3. Turn … up      6. gave up
        4. turned down

**Unit 12**

**12.1**  2. has
        3. goes
        4. does
        5. takes

**12.2**  2. He does the laundry every Saturday.
        3. She cleans the house every weekend.
        4. He watches TV/television sometimes.
        5. She goes for a walk every morning.

**12.3** *Possible answers:*
2. What time do you go to sleep? Usually at 10:30. / Usually I go to sleep at 10:30.
3. When do you check your e-mail? Every morning. / I check my e-mail every morning.
4. How often do you surf the Internet? Every night. / I surf the Internet every night.

## Unit 13

**13.1** *Possible answers:*
2. told      3. said      4. said; tell      5. tell      6. said
*Note: Other verb tenses may be possible; e.g., I will say goodbye to him.*

**13.2** 2. How do you say "tea" in Chinese?
3. Excuse me, can you tell me the time?   *or*   Can you tell me what time it is?
4. Can you tell me when the test is?
5. Do you speak English?

**13.3** 2. Say "house" in German
3. Ask for the check
4. Answer an e-mail
5. Say happy birthday
6. Talk to a friend
7. Ask someone to help you
*Note: We can say "answer an e-mail" but not "reply to the door!"*

**13.4** 1. ask; b      2. say; d      3. ask; a      4. say; c

## Unit 14

**14.1** *Possible answers:*
2. danced      4. run      6. fell      8. walk
3. swims      5. climb      7. jumped

**14.2** 2. flies      3. take      4. drives      5. take/ride      6. ride

**14.3** *Possible answers:*
2. Yes, I ride my bicycle twice a week.
3. I swim in the ocean once a year. I never swim in a pool.
4. I never jog. / I never go jogging.
5. I drive every day. / I drive a car every day.
6. I take the bus once a week.

**14.4** Ride:  bicycle, horse
Push:  door, shopping cart
Pass:  salt, milk, bread,
Catch: bus, plane

## Unit 15

**15.1** 2. and      3. but      4. So      5. although

**15.2** *Possible sentences:*
Mary agreed to marry Paul after they decided to go into business together.
Mary will marry Paul although she doesn't love him.
Mary agreed to marry Paul, and they had two sons.

Mary agreed to marry Paul because he was a rock star.
Mary will marry Paul before he moves to Hollywood.
Mary will marry Paul, but she doesn't love him.
Mary agreed to marry Paul if he moved to Hollywood.
Mary agreed to marry Paul, so he moved to Hollywood.
Mary will marry Paul when he moves to Hollywood.

**15.3**  1. too/also    2. even    3. like    4. than    5. only

**15.4**  *Possible answers:*
I only play tennis in the summer.
It is too cold to swim here, even in summer.
I like listening to music, and I also like reading.
I like going skiing, too.
I go skiing a lot with my children, and sometimes my husband also comes.

**15.5**  *Possible answers:*
1. … I enjoy it.
2. … I do all the exercises in this book.
3. … I am also studying French.
4. … it is difficult at times.
5. … I was 12.
6. … I can understand some English-language movies.

**Unit 16**

**16.1**  2. a century    3. a week    4. a year

**16.2**
| | | | |
|---|---|---|---|
| 1. Monday | 4. Saturday | 7. April | 10. September |
| 2. August | 5. Wednesday | 8. Thursday | 11. Tuesday |
| 3. October | 6. January | 9. February | 12. November |

**16.3**

| Number of days in the month | Month |
|---|---|
| 30 | April, June, September, November |
| 31 | January, March, May, July, August, October, December |
| 28/29 | February |

**16.4**  1. T F S (first letters of the days of the week)
2. A S O N D (first letters of the months)

**16.5**  I'm going to a party on <u>S</u>aturday for Jill's birthday. Her birthday is on <u>T</u>uesday, but she wanted to have the party on the <u>w</u>eekend. She's having a barbecue. I think spring is a good time to have a party because of the weather. I love going to barbecues <u>in</u> the spring. My birthday is in <u>w</u>inter, and it's too cold to eat outside!

**16.6**  *Possible answers:*
It is possible here to give answers to only some of these questions. Check with your teacher if you are not sure of the answers to any of the other questions.
5. July
7. Sunday, Saturday, Friday, Thursday, Wednesday, Tuesday, Monday
8. 30 minutes
10. afternoon

**Unit 17**

**17.1**  2. for  3. from  4. to  5. At  6. for

**17.2**  1. Probably tomorrow.
2. Probably a week ago.
3. In a few minutes.

**17.3**  *Possible answers:*
2. Sometimes I take the bus to school. I usually drive.
3. I never play soccer.
4. I always watch TV on Saturday.
5. Sometimes I drink milk. Usually I drink coffee.
6. I never wear a hat.
7. I often eat chocolate.
8. I sometimes go to bed at 10. I usually go to bed at 11.
9. I sometimes go to the movies.

**17.4**  Stefan plays tennis twice a week. He practices the piano once a week. He has a business meeting in Toronto once a month. Alicia and Amy play tennis three times a week. They practice the piano twice a day. They go to Toronto for a business meeting six times a year.   *or*   They have business meetings in Toronto six times a year.

**17.5**  *Possible answer:*
I usually get up early. I always have a cup of coffee when I wake up. I often work at home, but sometimes I go to school to teach. I never drive. Sometimes I walk to school, and sometimes I take the bus. Sometimes I have lunch in a park near school. I usually eat a sandwich. Sometimes I have an apple, too, but I hardly ever have a hot lunch. Once a week I visit a friend and we go to the movies together or have lunch in a restaurant.

**Unit 18**

**18.1**  1. c  2. a  3. d  4. b  5. f  6. e

**18.2**

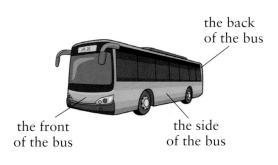
the back
of the bus

the front
of the bus

the side
of the bus

the top
of the tree

the bottom
of the tree

**18.3**  1. overseas  3. away / out of town
2. out  4. away; overseas

**18.4**  *Possible answers:*
2. Yes, I'm going to Canada and to the U.S.
3. I have a pen in my right hand.
4. The unit on **Have** is at the beginning of this book (Unit 3). Note *at.*
5. The unit on **Feelings** is in the middle of this book (Unit 35). Note *in.*

## Unit 19

**19.1**
2. badly/poorly
3. loudly
4. fast (*not* ~~fastly~~)
5. quietly
6. well

**19.2** *Possible answers:*
2. Most people like a fast bus.
3. Usually it's better to speak softly.
4. A right answer is best in class!
5. It's usually better to work quickly.
6. It's better to sing well.

**19.3**

**19.4**

| Word | Definition | (✓) Right   (✗) Wrong |
|------|------------|------------------------|
| suddenly | very slowly | ✗ |
| sadly | in an unhappy way | ✓ |
| strangely | not in a normal way | ✓ |
| quickly | very slowly | ✗ |
| easily | with no difficulty | ✓ |

*Suddenly* means very quickly, when you are not expecting it.
*Quickly* is similar to *fast* when *fast* is an adverb (e.g., He runs *fast*.), not when it is an adjective.

**19.5** *Possible answers:*
My cousin runs fast. My mother is very friendly.
My aunt is a quiet person. My father drives well.
My brother speaks slowly. I'm a fast runner.

## Unit 20

**20.1**

| Base form | Past tense | Past participle | Opposite |
|-----------|-----------|-----------------|----------|
| win/find | won/found | won/found | **lose** |
| **throw** | threw | thrown | catch |
| sit | sat | **sat** | stand |
| begin | **began** | begun | end/stop |
| buy | bought | bought | **sell** |

**20.2** *Possible answers:*
2. ate/had
3. made/had/drank
4. read
5. drove/went
6. sent/wrote
7. ran/jogged
8. bought
9. sat
10. made
11. left
12. met
13. went
14. slept

**20.3** *Possible answers:*
2. been  5. known
3. had/eaten  6. seen
4. read

## Unit 21
**21.1** 2. milk; butter  4. traffic
3. advice  5. work

**21.2**

| Countable nouns | Uncountable nouns |
|---|---|
| banana | advice |
| book | butter |
| car | coffee |
| cup | furniture |
| pen | information |
| shirt | milk |
| teacher | money |
| train | news |
| | rice |
| | traffic |
| | work |

**21.3** 2. is/was  4. was  6. are  8. is
3. are/were  5. is; was / will be; was  7. is

**21.4** 2. I'd like some <u>information</u> about your country.
3. Let me give you <u>some</u> advice.
4. Cook <u>this</u> rice for 30 minutes.
5. Maria is looking for a new <u>job</u>.  *or*  Maria is looking for new work.
6. There's usually better weather in the east than in the west.
7. We should buy some new <u>furniture</u>.
8. I saw <u>a lot of</u> traffic on my way to school.

## Unit 22
**22.1** *Possible answers:*
2. better than
3. terrible/awful/bad
4. excellent/great/wonderful
5. awful/terrible
6. great/wonderful/terrific
7. worse than

**22.2** *Possible answers:*
2. Oh, how awful!
3. That's a great/good idea.
4. Yes, there's Nakajima. It's the best restaurant in town.
5. S/he's a wonderful/terrific person! (We hope you can say this!)
6. That's terrible/awful.

**22.3** 2. e  3. a  4. b  5. d

**148**

**22.4**

| *Good* | *Bad* |
|---|---|
| awesome | horrible |
| fantastic | mean |
| fine | nasty |
| gorgeous | |
| super | |

**22.5** *Possible answers*
fantastic weather / fantastic music
a fine wine / a fine time
a gorgeous view / gorgeous clothes
a super idea / a super dinner
a nasty person / a nasty cold
a mean man / a mean letter
a horrible accident / a horrible feeling

## Unit 23

**23.1** *Possible answers:*
1. A: Alan's very nice.
   B: He's more than nice, he's **wonderful/terrific!**
2. A: George wasn't very nice to you, was he?
   B: No, he was really **mean/awful!**
3. A: Hank doesn't like to give things to other people.
   B: Yes, he seems **selfish.**
4. A: Is your little brother smart?
   B: Yes, he's very **smart/intelligent.**

**23.2** smart; terrific; friendly; kind; happy; good; wonderful; stupid; terrible

**23.3** Most people probably think they are most of these things at some time, or at least the positive ones!

*Possible answers:*
I am very *friendly* and *kind to animals*.
I am *nice to my friends* and others.
I think I am *smart*.
I have a *terrific* brother.

**23.4** 2. of     3. to     4. of

### Unit 24
**24.1** 2. e     3. a     4. f     5. g     6. b     7. d

**24.2** *Possible answers:*
1. an e-mail address; glasses; a phone number
2. a word; an e-mail address; a phone number
3. dinner; the movie; the party; a vacation
4. pictures

**24.3** *Possible answers:*
1. I was good at languages and bad at art.
2. I'm good at tennis and swimming.
3. I am proud of my family.
4. I am afraid of going to the dentist.
5. I like listening to jazz. / I listen to jazz.
6. I am looking forward to my vacation.
7. I am interested in traveling to different places.

### Unit 25
**25.1** 2. rewrite/redo     4. unhappy     6. unsafe
      3. informal       5. misbehave

**25.2** *Possible answers:*
  2. rice that has been cooked
  3. a wrong answer, an answer that is not correct
  4. read a book again
  5. to tell a story again
  6. a word that is not spelled correctly
  7. an e-mail that is not finished
  8. an area where you cannot smoke
  9. someone who is no longer with his girlfriend
10. a task that cannot be done

**25.3** 2. e     3. f     4. c     5. a     6. b

*Possible answers:*
2. His answer was incomplete.
3. I need to repaint my room.
4. Don't misjudge people.
5. I always buy nonfat milk.
6. Never leave test questions unanswered.

**25.4** 2. uncomfortable     5. inconsiderate     8. incorrect
      3. unfriendly         6. unsure
      4. inconvenient     7. impolite

**Unit 26**

26.1    2. instructor      4. stapler         6. happiness
         3. swimmer      5. calculator

26.2    1. e      2. a      3. d      4. c      5. b

26.3    *Possible answers:*
       (You may be able to think of some other possible combinations.)
       2. sunny beach/weather/smile
       3. useful car/idea/book
       4. useless car/book/picture
       5. sandy beach
       6. endless beach/book

26.4    *Possible answers:*
       2. the state of feeling lonely
       3. the opposite of quickly
       4. with lots of hope
       5. weather when it is raining
       6. It doesn't hurt.
       7. the opposite of doing something well
       8. a thing (or gadget) for opening cans
       9. full of clouds
     10. a person who surfs

**Unit 27**

27.1    *Possible answers:*
       2. Good luck!
       3. Congratulations!
       4. Goodbye. / See you soon. / Take care.
       5. Happy Birthday!
       6. You're welcome.
       7. Hello! / Hi!
       8. Thank you. / Thanks.

27.2    1. Excuse me!
       2. Congratulations!
       3. Happy New Year!
       4. Good morning.
       5. I'm sorry!
       6. Good night. / Take care. / See you soon.

27.3    *Possible answers:*
       2. Good night. Sleep well.
       3. Good morning. (also: Hello.)
       4. I'm sorry.
       5. Happy New Year!
       6. Excuse me, I didn't understand what you said.

27.4    1. ANN:   Hi!
       2. BILL:   Hi, how are you?
       3. ANN:   Fine, thanks. Today's my birthday.
       4. BILL:   Happy Birthday!

1. TOMOKO:  Do you want something to drink?
2. MICHAEL:  Yes, please.
3. TOMOKO:  Would you like lemonade? I just made some.
4. MICHAEL:  Thanks!

**27.5** *Possible answers:*
A: Good morning.
B: Hi. How are you?
A: Fine, thanks. How about you?
B: Pretty good, but I'm a little nervous. I'm taking my driving test today.
A: Good luck. That's funny, I passed mine last week.
B: Oh, congratulations!

A: It's my birthday today.
B: It is? Happy Birthday! Why don't we go out and celebrate this evening?
A: OK. See you later.
B: See you soon.

## Unit 28

**28.1**  1. its      3. their     5. They're
      2. You're    4. It's      6. your

**28.2**  1. d    2. c    3. b    4. e    5. a

**28.3**  2. used to live     4. is used to eating     6. used to work
      3. used to sell     5. is used to driving

*Possible answers:*

**28.4**

| *I used to do this.* | *I'm used to doing this.* |
| --- | --- |
| I used to play outside all day. | Now, I'm used to working at a desk all day. |
| I used to get up at noon. | Now, I'm used to getting up at 7 o'clock. |
| I used to rollerskate. | Now, I'm used to driving everywhere. |

## Unit 29

**29.1**  2. Mother Teresa was born in 1910 and died in 1997.
      3. Benjamin Franklin was born in 1706 and died in 1790.
      4. Elvis Presley was born in 1935 and died in 1977.
      5. Leonardo da Vinci was born in 1452 and died in 1519.
      6. Martin Luther King, Jr., was born in 1929 and died in 1968.

**29.2**  1. died     3. dead     5. dead
      2. death   4. died

**29.3**  2. a (bride)groom     5. divorced         8. a widow (woman)
      3. single            6. a funeral
      4. a baby           7. a honeymoon

**29.4**  1. married     3. wedding     5. death     7. named
      2. died        4. honeymoon   6. born      8. birthday

**29.5** *Possible answer:*

I have two brothers and two sisters. My sisters are both married. One sister got married this year. She was a beautiful bride. They went to Hawaii on their honeymoon. The other sister got married four years ago. She has two children – the boy was born two years ago, and the girl was born last year. One of my brothers is divorced and one is single. My father died two years ago. My mother is a widow.

## Unit 30

**30.1**

| | |
|---|---|
| 2. brother | 8. niece |
| 3. aunt | 9. mother |
| 4. uncle | 10. wife |
| 5. grandmother | 11. cousin |
| 6. grandfather | 12. grandson |
| 7. nephew | |

**30.2** *Possible family tree:*

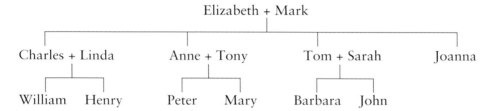

I am Tony. Anne is my wife. Peter and Mary are our children. Peter is our son, and Mary is our daughter. Barbara is our niece. William, Henry, and John are our nephews.

**30.3**

| | | |
|---|---|---|
| 1. e | 3. b | 5. d |
| 2. a | 4. c | |

**30.4** *Possible answers:*

1. Chen has one brother and no sisters.
2. Chen has two cousins.
3. Chen has two nephews, but he doesn't have any nieces.
4. Chen has only one grandmother now.
5. Chen has three aunts and two uncles.

## Unit 31

**31.1**

| | |
|---|---|
| 2. feet | 7. brain/head |
| 3. eyes | 8. blood |
| 4. nose | 9. legs/feet |
| 5. toes | 10. face |
| 6. ears | |

**31.2**

| | |
|---|---|
| 2. football | 5. earrings |
| 3. lipstick | 6. backpack |
| 4. hairbrush | |

**31.3**

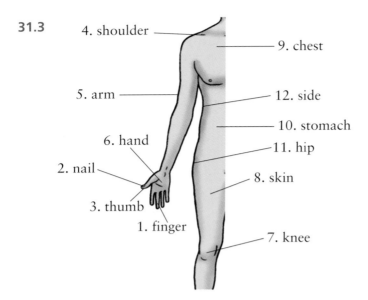

4. shoulder
9. chest
5. arm
12. side
10. stomach
6. hand
11. hip
2. nail
8. skin
3. thumb
1. finger
7. knee

**Unit 32**

**32.1**
2. jacket    5. sweater    8. suit
3. socks    6. scarf    9. shorts
4. belt    7. shirt    10. umbrella

**32.2**
1. foot – shoe    3. eyes – glasses    5. head – hat
2. hand – glove    4. waist – belt    6. neck – scarf

**32.3**
1. are; is    4. had; carried    7. Is
2. wore    5. is; are    8. get dressed
3. put; took    6. were; are

**32.4**
2. sweater    7. shirt (also: blouse)
3. gloves    8. coat
4. skirt    9. briefcase
5. boots    10. umbrella
6. hat    11. purse

**32.5** *Possible answer:*
I am wearing a blue T-shirt and black pants. I have white shoes on. I'm also
wearing gloves and a pair of glasses.

**Unit 33**

**33.1**
2. tall    4. light/fair    6. overweight/fat
3. slim/thin    5. young    7. elderly

**33.2** *Possible answers:*
2. Is Elena's hair blonde/fair/light?
3. What color are Mike's eyes?
4. Are your parents old? (or more polite: Are your parents elderly?)
5. How much does Hiromi weigh?

**33.3** *Possible answers:*
1. Sue has long blonde hair and fair/light skin.
2. Jeff has dark skin and short black hair.
3. Wendy has long dark hair.
4. Dick's hair is long, and he has a beard and a mustache.

**33.4** *Possible answers:*
Lisa: Lisa is tall. She has long black hair and brown eyes. She's very pretty.

Kevin: Kevin is average height. He has brown hair and a beard. His eyes are blue. He's kind of ordinary looking.

My mother: My mother is short, with gray hair. She has green eyes. She is a beautiful woman.

## Unit 34
**34.1** *Possible answers:*

| Not very serious | Somewhat serious | Very serious |
|---|---|---|
| a headache<br>a toothache<br>a cough<br>a cold | allergies<br>asthma<br>throwing up | cancer<br>a heart attack |

*Note: The health problems labeled "not very serious" and "somewhat serious" can become very serious if they are not treated.*

**34.2** *Possible answers:*
1. (I'm) fine, thanks. / Good, how are you?
2. I feel sick. or I don't feel good.
3. I feel sick. or I don't feel very good.
4. I have a toothache.
5. a cold?

**34.3** 2. heart attack     3. allergies     4. cancer / heart attacks

**34.4** *Possible answers:*
1. A good diet means eating a lot of fruit and vegetables, and not too many sweets.
2. I like/love swimming / cycling / playing golf / skiing / jogging / playing tennis.
3. Sometimes I have a lot of stress at work / when I have tests.
4. Yes, I had an operation once / I broke my leg. (*Note*: "Be in the hospital" means you are a patient, staying in a hospital. "Be in a hospital" can mean that you are a patient or that you are visiting someone.)

## Unit 35
**35.1** *Possible answers:*
2. I hate cooking.
3. I like driving on sunny days.
4. I love chocolate!
5. I love soccer!
6. I don't like cats.

7. I like dancing.
8. I don't like jazz.

**35.2**  *Possible answers:*
2. I hope (that) the class ends soon.
3. I want something to eat / some food.
4. I hope (that) my friend feels better soon.
5. I want to go to bed / go to sleep.
6. I hope to see my friend soon.   *or*   I hope (that) we see each other soon.

**35.3**  2. Fred is thirsty.
3. The children are happy.
4. Bob is tired.
5. Mr. Lee is cold.
6. Mrs. Jones is angry.

**35.4**  *Possible answers:*
2. I felt surprised yesterday when an old friend called me.
3. I felt angry when my boss was rude to me.
4. I felt sad when I dropped my ice cream.
*Note: You can also say: I was surprised; I was angry; I was sad.*

**Unit 36**

**36.1**  2. The Alps are in Europe.
3. The Amazon River is in South America.
4. The Great Barrier Reef is in Australia.
5. The Great Wall is in Asia.
6. The Andes Mountains are in South America.
7. The Nile River is in Africa.
8. Mount Fuji is in Asia.
9. The Grand Canyon is in North America.

**36.2**

| 2. d | 5. j | 8. f |
|------|------|-------|
| 3. g | 6. i | 9. b |
| 4. h | 7. a | 10. c |

**36.3**  Check your answers with your teacher or a reference book (such as an atlas or dictionary) if you are not sure.

**36.4**

| 2. Thai | 5. Mexican | 8. Peruvian | 11. Indonesian |
|---------|-----------|-------------|----------------|
| 3. Brazilian | 6. Filipino | 9. Chinese | 12. Chilean |
| 4. Canadian | 7. French | 10. Vietnamese | |

**36.5**  2. In Mexico, Spain, and Panama they speak Spanish, but in Brazil they speak Portuguese.
3. In Austria, Germany, and Switzerland they speak German, but in Italy they speak Italian.
4. In Egypt, Saudi Arabia and Algeria they speak Arabic, but in South Africa they do not. (There are 11 official languages in South Africa, including English and Afrikaans.)

**Unit 37**

**37.1**

| 1. e | 3. g | 5. f | 7. c |
|------|------|------|------|
| 2. d | 4. a | 6. b | |

**37.2** *Possible answers:*

most favorite ←――――――――→ least favorite
snow, sun, wind, rain, lightning, cloud, fog

**37.3**  3. It is / It's cloudy in Caracas.
4. It is / It's snowing   *or*   It is / It's snowy in London.
5. It is / It's foggy in Seoul.
6. It is / It's windy in Toronto.

**37.4**  2. rains / is raining
3. weather
4. snowing/snowy
5. lightning
6. storm/thunderstorm/hurricane
7. forecast

**37.5** *Possible answers:*

1. It usually snows in December.
2. It is usually 70 degrees Fahrenheit (21 degrees Celsius) in summer and 32 degrees Fahrenheit (0 degrees Celsius) in winter.
3. Sometimes there are thunderstorms in August.
4. It is not usually wet in spring.
5. We almost never have hurricanes.
6. Summer is my favorite season because it is warm and dry.

**37.6** *Possible answer:*

Today it is sunny and warm. There are just a few clouds in the sky and a little wind. It is not raining, and it is not snowing. There is no thunder or lightning.

## Unit 38

**38.1**  2. At the tourist information office.
3. At the bank.
4. In/At the parking garage.
5. At the museum.
6. At the Internet café.
7. At the bookstore.
8. At the library.

**38.2** *Possible answers:*

2. Where's the post office?
3. How do I get to the art museum?
4. Where can I park?
5. Where can I change money?   *or*   Is there a bank nearby?

**38.3** *Possible answers:*

2. at a store
3. at the library
4. on the street   *or*   in a police station
5. in a bank

**38.4**  1. Railroad crossing
2. Bus stop
3. No parking (Do not leave your car here.)
4. Do not enter
5. Airport ahead

**38.5**  *Possible answer:*
I live in a small town. There are not many places to see in town, but there is a nice art museum and a wonderful bookstore. You can also go to the library and see special exhibits.

## Unit 39

**39.1**  1. mountains          5. fields          9. tractor
2. hills          6. road          10. forest
3. woods          7. river          11. lake
4. farm          8. path/trail          12. town/village

**39.2**  *Possible answers:*
1. farmer; on          5. lake/river (also: pond, swimming pool)
2. cabin          6. wildlife
3. town/village          7. path/trail
4. mountains

**39.3**  *Possible answer:*
There are some big forests and a lot of farms. There are no hills or mountains. The countryside is flat. There are lots of trails where you can walk. There is one big river and there are some small rivers. The wildlife there is very beautiful. There are a lot of small towns.

**39.4**  2. He loves nature.
3. She wants to live in the country.
4. They are interested in wildlife.
5. She likes to paint pictures of the countryside.

## Unit 40

**40.1**  *Possible answers:*
2. giraffe
3. Parrots; parakeets; chickens
4. Tigers; lions
5. horse; elephant
6. Fish; birds
7. meat
8. Chickens; cows (or pigs)

**40.2**  2. e          3. a          4. c          5. b

**40.3**  *Possible answers:*
1. Lions, tigers, monkeys, snakes, dogs, and cats
2. Cows, sheep, pigs, parrots (for feathers), and snakes (for snakeskin)
   (You may think of some other things, e.g., horsehair for certain wigs).
3. Chickens, turtles, parrots, parakeets, snakes, and fish
4. Cats, parakeet, turtle
5. Monkeys, snakes

**40.4**

**40.5** Write down the number you remembered correctly. Try again tomorrow and write down how many you remember then.

**Unit 41**

**41.1**
| | | |
|---|---|---|
| 2. d | 5. c | 8. g |
| 3. i | 6. j | 9. a |
| 4. f | 7. b | 10. h |

**41.2** *Possible answers:*
1. A one-way ticket takes you to a place, and a round-trip ticket takes you to a place and back.
2. You get your luggage/baggage.
3. No, it lands at the end of a trip and takes off at the beginning of a trip.
4. If you rent a car, you use it for a day or a week and then return it. If you buy a car, it is your car.
5. You give your luggage to the airline to put on the plane for you.
6. No, carry on means that you didn't check any bags.

**41.3**

**Unit 42**

**42.1**  1. c  2. a  3. d  4. b

**42.2**  1. d  2. c  3. b  4. a

**42.3**  *Possible answers:*
No Smoking – in public places (e.g., restaurant, theater, government offices, store, elevator)
No Parking – on the street
Entrance and Exit – in a theater, museum, meeting hall, etc.
Exit – in an airport, theater, stadium, parking garage, etc.
Caution: Wet Floor – in a public restroom (toilet)
Pay Here – in a store or restaurant
Push and Pull – on doors in public places (e.g., store, train station, museum)
Sale – on a store window, on a display inside a store
Open and Closed – on the door of a store, restaurant, or museum
Keep off the Grass – in some parks, on the lawn (grass) outside a public building
Men/Women or Gentlemen/Ladies – in a restaurant, airport, theater, park, etc.
Restrooms – same as Men/Women

**Unit 43**

**43.1**  2. (French) fries
3. pasta
4. hamburger(s)
5. dessert(s)
6. any two of the following: hamburgers, hot dogs, pizza, (French) fries
7. Pizza
8. bread/cakes

**43.2**

| Fruit | Vegetables |
|---|---|
| pineapple | green bean |
| grape | carrot |
| apple | onion |
| orange | garlic |
| banana | mushroom |
| pear | |

*Possible additions:*

| Fruit | Vegetables |
|---|---|
| strawberry | pea |
| kiwi | potato |
| peach | lettuce |
| | celery |

**43.3**

**43.4** *Possible answer:*
My three favorite foods are vegetables, pasta, and desserts. My three favorite drinks are tea, orange juice, and water. All of my favorite foods and drinks are good for me except maybe the desserts.

### Unit 44

**44.1**

| Check (✓) yes or no. | *yes* | *no* |
|---|---|---|
| 1. I use a frying pan to drink out of. | | ✓ |
| 2. Dish soap makes the dishes clean. | ✓ | |
| 3. The refrigerator is cold inside. | ✓ | |
| 4. The freezer is not as cold as the refrigerator. | | ✓ |
| 5. I turn on the faucet to get water. | ✓ | |
| 6. A dishtowel is for making plates wet. | | ✓ |
| 7. You can use paper towels to clean the counter. | ✓ | |

The freezer is colder than the refrigerator.
A dishtowel makes plates dry.

**44.2** *Possible answers:*
2. I need tea, a teapot, a cup, and a spoon.
3. I need an egg, a frying pan, butter or oil, and a stove.
4. I need a plate or a bowl, a knife and fork, or a spoon, or chopsticks.
5. I need water and a glass, or a cup, or a mug.
6. I need a microwave.

**44.3** *Possible answers:*
2. B: Yes, it's in the refrigerator.
3. B: It goes in the cabinet/cupboard.
4. A: Where's the ice? / Where can I find the ice?
5. B: Yes, it's next to the stove.
6. B: It's in the oven.

### Unit 45

**45.1**
1. mirror          4. pajamas          7. alarm clock
2. closet          5. pillow           8. night table / nightstand
3. dresser         6. table lamp       9. bed

**45.2** *Possible answers:*
toothpaste, hairbrush, comb, pajamas or nightgown, shampoo

**45.3**
2. Aya is washing her face.
3. Mr. and Mrs. Park are having/eating breakfast.
4. Luis is taking a shower.
5. James is getting dressed.
6. Antonio is turning off the light.   *or*   Antonio is going to bed.

**45.4** *Possible answer:*
I usually go to bed at 10 p.m. I am usually tired, but I always read for a while. I turn off the light after 10 minutes. I fall asleep quickly. I wake up before my alarm clock rings, but I don't get out of bed. I get up when my alarm clock rings at 6 a.m. I take a shower, brush my teeth, and get dressed. I go to the kitchen and eat breakfast.

## Unit 46

**46.1** *Possible answers:*

2. a sofa/couch
3. a coffee table, an end table
4. a picture
5. a light switch
6. a stereo
7. a carpet

**46.2** 1. (c)  2. (b)  3. (a)  4. (b)

**46.3** 2. in; on  3. near / next to  4. against  5. under

**46.4** *Possible answer:*

In my living room there is a brown sofa, a table, a TV, a desk, and two armchairs. The sofa is against the wall, and the TV is near the window. The table is in the middle of the room. The walls are white, and there are some pictures on them. I like to relax in the living room. In the evening I watch TV there or listen to music.

## Unit 47

**47.1** 1. lawyer  3. hairdresser  5. farmer
2. mechanic  4. receptionist  6. nurse

**47.2**

**47.3** 2. mechanic  3. salesclerk  4. nurse  5. hairdresser

**47.4** *Possible answers:*

1. I'm a student.
2. I go to West College.
3. Yes, it's very interesting.

## Unit 48

**48.1** 2. d  5. b  8. a
3. g  6. i  9. j
4. f  7. e  10. h

**48.2** notebook, pencil, eraser, ruler, paper clip, pen, pencil sharpener, stapler

**48.3**   2. does          5. taking          8. passes
          3. passes          6. take          9. get (also: receive)
          4. studies or takes   7. take          10. fails

**48.4**   *Possible answer*:
          My favorite subjects are English and art. I like to write and draw pictures.
          I don't like physics, chemistry, and math. These are very difficult for me.

**Unit 49**

**49.1**   1. Maggie          3. Andrew          5. Real Suppliers / Robin
          2. Soccer practice   4. (555) 485-9684   6. Oct 12, 2010

**49.2**   1. message     2. fax     3. text     4. e-mail / e-mail message

**49.3**   *Possible answers*:

|  | Write an e-mail | Send a fax | Write a letter | Make a phone call | Send a text message |
|---|---|---|---|---|---|
| parents | O | N | S | O | N |
| professors | O | N | N | S | N |
| restaurant | N | N | N | S | N |
| government office | S | S | S | S | N |
| friends | O | N | S | O | O |

**Unit 50**

**50.1**   1. (b)     2. (c)     3. (b)     4. (a)

**50.2**   2. luggage     3. passport     4. currency     5. camera     6. ticket(s)

**50.3**   1. c     2. d     3. e     4. f     5. a     6. b

**50.4**   *Possible answers*:
          1. A car is usually faster.
          2. It is usually cheaper to take the bus, especially for a family.
          3. You can take more luggage on a ferry.
          4. You can see more from a car, in most cases.

**Unit 51**

**51.1**   1. drugstore     3. hardware store     5. gift shop
          2. toy store     4. electronics store     6. bakery

**51.2**   2. a department store     5. a grocery store / a supermarket
          3. a post office          6. a bookstore
          4. a gift shop

**51.3**   1. fourth floor          4. food and sports equipment
          2. cosmetics          5. second floor
          3. Garden Restaurant / fifth floor   6. stationery

**51.4**  2. cash or bills      4. the cashier / cash register      6. change
        3. a credit card      5. a receipt

**51.5**  1. cost      3. larger size      5. bag / shopping bag
        2. try      4. use / pay by

## Unit 52

**52.1**  2. nonsmoking      5. coffeemaker      8. elevator
        3. Internet connection      6. floor      9. luggage
        4. television/TV      7. room key      10. bill

**52.2**  2. a      5. b      8. e
        3. i      6. j      9. h
        4. f      7. c      10. g

**52.3**  *Possible answers:*

| Service | A cheap hotel | An average hotel | A luxury hotel |
|---|---|---|---|
| room service | | ✓ | ✓ |
| wake-up call | ✓ | ✓ | ✓ |
| valet parking | | | ✓ |
| Internet connection | | ✓ | ✓ |
| concierge | | | ✓ |
| dry cleaning | | | ✓ |

**52.4**  *Possible answers:*
Can I have a wake-up call, please?
Can I have room service, please?
Can I reserve a room for next week, please?
Can I have a double room for tonight, please?
Can I have my bill, please?
Can I have a hair dryer, please?

## Unit 53

**53.1**  *Possible answers:*
        1. c      3. b      5. d
        2. e      4. a

**53.2**  *Possible answers:*
café – Corner Café
restaurant – The Second Street Grill
coffee shop – Athens Coffee Shop
deli – the New York Stage Deli
fast-food restaurant – Burger King

**53.3**  *Possible answers:*
        1. I'd order the New York steak as an entree.
        2. A vegetarian might choose fried mushrooms, tomato or French onion soup, the pasta primavera, a green salad, or any of the beverages and desserts.
        3. Four things made with chicken are chicken wings, chicken soup, grilled chicken breast, and chicken salad.
        4. Cola is a soft drink.

**53.4**  2. beverage    5. steak
         3. salad       6. ice cream
         4. potato

**53.5**  WAITER:     Are you ready **to** order?
         CUSTOMER:  Yes. **I'd like** the French onion soup and a hamburger, please.
         WAITER:     **How** would you like your hamburger? Rare, medium, or **well-
                    done**?
         CUSTOMER:  Medium.
         WAITER:     Anything to drink?
         CUSTOMER:  **I'll have** an iced tea, please.

**Unit 54**
**54.1**  2. sailing      5. ice skating
         3. tennis       6. swimming
         4. soccer

**54.2**  1. tennis            4. table tennis (Ping-Pong)
         2. basketball        5. golf
         3. baseball          6. skiing

**54.3**  *Possible answers:*
         2. What's your favorite sport?
         3. Do you play any sports?
         4. Do you go swimming / like swimming / swim?

**54.4**  1. c     2. d     3. e     4. b     5. a

**54.5**  *Possible answer:*
         I played baseball, but I did not like it. I also played basketball, and I liked
         it a lot.
         I would like to try soccer.

**Unit 55**
**55.1**  2. science fiction          6. romantic comedy / a love story / romantic
         3. horror                   7. detective
         4. action                   8. musical
         5. cartoon / animated film

**55.2**
         T H R I L L E R
            H O R R O R
          C O M E D Y
              A C T I O N
     S C I E N C E F I C T I O N
        W E S T E R N
        M U S I C A L
            C A R T O O N

**55.3** *Possible answers:*
1. to (the)
2. watched (also: saw or rented)
3. played
4. in
5. movie stars
6. director

**55.4** *Possible answers:*
1. *Star Wars*, *Star Trek*, *Alien*, etc.
2. Harrison Ford, Julia Roberts, Cameron Diaz, Antonio Banderas, Jackie Chan, etc.
3. Yes, I love them.   or No, they're boring. *Dick Tracy* is one example.
4. Yes, if I'm not alone.
5. This week a James Bond movie is playing.

## Unit 56

**56.1** Possible answers:
1. She's watching TV.
2. He's gardening.
3. He's reading the newspaper.
4. She's cooking.
5. She's using the Internet. / She's on the Internet. / She's using a computer.
6. He's listening to music.

**56.2**

| | |
|---|---|
| 2. talk | 6. see/watch |
| 3. take | 7. see/watch |
| 4. have/invite | 8. grows |
| 5. play | 9. record |

**56.3** *Possible answers:*
1. We talk or have a meal, or we listen to music.
2. I like to download classical music.
3. I like novels, and I read the newspaper every day.
4. I text them almost every day, sometimes a few times a day.
5. We like to watch movies and play games.
6. Yes, I have three houseplants in my room.

**56.4** *Possible answers:*

Most interesting                                                                                          Most boring

←——————————————————————————————————————————————————————→

| surfing the Web | watching TV | listening to music | reading | doing nothing | cooking | gardening |

## Unit 57

**57.1**

| | |
|---|---|
| 2. (bank) robber | 4. burglar |
| 3. shoplifter | 5. (jewel) thief |

**57.2**

| | | |
|---|---|---|
| 2. vandals | 4. fine | 6. burglaries |
| 3. speeding | 5. innocent | 7. hacker |

**57.3** *Possible answers:*

Most serious　　　　　　　　　　　　　　　　　　　　　　Least serious

←───────────────────────────────────────────────────→

| 2 | 3 | 6 | 5 | 4 | 1 | 7 |

## Unit 58

**58.1**
2. documentary (also: program)　　5. teen
3. fashion　　　　　　　　　　　　6. Internet
4. nature　　　　　　　　　　　　7. comic books / comics

**58.2**
1. e　　3. b　　5. c
2. d　　4. a

**58.3**

| Computer magazines | Women's magazines | News magazines | Teen magazines |
|---|---|---|---|
| news about the Internet | articles about health, diet, family<br><br>articles about interesting women | interviews with the president<br><br>articles on the economy | pictures of pop musicians |

**58.4**
2. a journalist　　　　　　　　4. a comic book / a comic
3. an evening (news)paper　　　5. a documentary

**58.5** *Possible answers:*
1. I always read a morning newspaper.
2. I get 203 channels.
3. I watch two or three hours every day.
4. I like documentaries and movies on TV. I like to listen to talk shows and music on the radio.

## Unit 59

**59.1**
2. She has too much work.　　　6. The room is messy.
3. Her computer crashed.　　　　7. The phone is out of order. / The phone
4. His hand is cut.　　　　　　　　isn't working.
5. The cup is broken.　　　　　　8. He is late for work.

**59.2** *Possible answers:*
2. finger / knees / hand
3. room / hair / desk
4. an appointment / class / work
5. camera / hair dryer / radio / washing machine / TV / computer
6. camera / hair dryer / radio / washing machine / TV / computer

**59.3**  *Possible answers:*

| Big problems | Small problems |
|---|---|
| late for work | a TV that doesn't work |
| a coffeemaker that isn't working | dying plants |
| a broken washing machine | a cut finger |
| an argument with a friend | a co-worker in a bad mood |
| a computer crash | a photocopier that is out of order |
| lost keys | a messy bedroom |
| too much work | |

**59.4**  *Possible answers:*
too much work – get an assistant
a co-worker in a bad mood – ignore it
a crashed computer – fix it
a photocopier that is out of order – call someone to fix it
a coffeemaker that isn't working – drink water

**59.5**  *Possible answers:*
My CD player doesn't work.
My brother lost his credit card.
My friend broke a glass.

## Unit 60
**60.1**
2. car crash
3. flood
4. war
5. earthquake
6. forest fire
7. hurricane
8. traffic jam
9. snowstorm

**60.2**  *Possible answers:*
homeless people, air pollution – in the big cities
floods – in the valleys, by the river

**60.3**
2. strike
3. War
4. accident
5. earthquakes; snowstorms
6. homeless
7. unemployed
8. rush hour